D0472267

The CUTTING EDGE
Home Dec Accents

Vivian Peritts

JACKSON COUNTY LIBRARY SERVICES
MEDFORD OREGON 97501

©2002 by Vivian Peritts
All rights reserved.

No portion of this publication may be reproduced or transmitted in any form or by any means, electronic or mechanical, including photocopy, recording, or any information storage and retrieval system, without permission in writing from the publisher, except by a reviewer who may quote brief passages in a critical article or review to be printed in a magazine or newspaper, or electronically transmitted on radio or television.

Published by

krause publications

700 East State Street • Iola, WI 54990-0001

Please call or write for our free catalog of publications. Our toll-free number to place an order or obtain a free catalog is (800) 258-0929.

Library of Congress Catalog Number: 2002105758
ISBN: 0-87349-499-7

Photography by April Fields and Vivian Peritts.

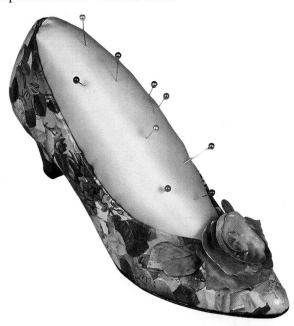

ACKNOWLEDGMENTS

This book was a wonderful adventure. The projects really were a joy to create. A God-given gift of creativity made this adventure possible. I never stop being amazed by the ideas that unfold in my head, purposely put there to be shared.

I would like to thank my family members for their patience with my schedule and the mess!

I am also grateful for my very talented friend and assistant Paula Heiney, who knows how my mind works and can read my writing. She has helped to make working on this book a pleasure.

Thank you April Fields for the beautiful photography, and to Steve Lam at S & J Studios for all of the step-by-step help and advice.

Talented friends created several projects in this book. Kimberly Martin was a creative force on many of the girl's room projects, and she's a great base coater, too! Pat Lingwall created the baby's room projects. Linda Baird constructed the House Lamp and helped in the production of several other projects. It takes a neighborhood to complete a book!

I would also like to thank acquisitions editor Julie Stephani and editor Maria Turner at Krause Publications for their confidence and support for this project.

Many of these projects are the result of my work with Jim Booth at Emagination Crafts, Inc. His great punches and papers were the inspiration for many of the projects.

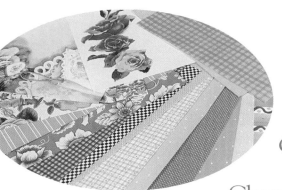

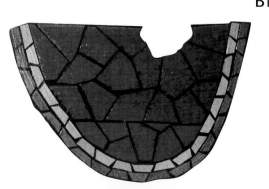

INTRODUCTION

Scrapbooking has become a huge industry. Today, there are entire stores specializing in scrapbooking supplies and equipment, and there are probably few households in the United States that don't have some of these items in a drawer. We scrapbook enthusiasts have spent a fortune to keep up our collections. So isn't it great to find new ways to use those scrapbooking tools?

I know exactly how it goes. You have been personalizing your scrapbooks. Each page has been carefully thought out and planned. Each design is different and reflects your taste and sense of style. You have become very familiar with the tools and feel comfortable using them. These tools take up room, and you have a lot invested in them. So why not expand upon their uses? Think beyond the page.

Creating home décor is a new way to grow. You have a feel for expanding yourself on a small scale, so look for inspiration on these pages to try some large venues for your talents. Don't limit yourself to just the page—try a whole room.

Within this book, you will see products that your equipment works well with. All of the supplies you have been collecting, as well as those extra photos you have stashed, can now be used in new and exciting ways. Take your themes off the page and use them as themes for a room.

I loved working on this book because I felt comfortable with the tools and techniques, and you will, too. I hope you enjoy these projects as much as I do!

CHAPTER 1 EQUIPMENT

COMPUTER

Your computer is a great tool. It gives you the opportunity to manipulate photos, and add mats and borders. It also gives you thousands of fonts from which to choose your lettering.

Your computer probably came with a type of drawing program (Microsoft Paint, for example) and a word processing program (Works, Word, Word Perfect, etc.). With just these two types of programs, you can print your own decorative papers and titles, as well as copy your photos.

Other programs that are useful are desktop publishing like Print Shop and Publisher. These programs give more options for title and page designs.

Then there are programs for working with photographs, such as MGI Photosuite and Microsoft Photo Editor.

Look at the programs that came with your computer, your scanner, and even your printer. Play with these programs and see where they can lead you.

CRAFT KNIFE AND MAT

A sharp blade is important when using a craft knife, so be sure to have a good supply of new blades. And to protect your working surface, always use a self-healing mat on your cutting surface.

CRIMPERS

Straight lines or wavy lines can be crimped into paper by passing it through these handheld tools. Hold the handle tightly and crank. See how many ways you can think of to use this great tool.

DIE-CUTTER

Use the large die-cut machine in your local scrapbooking store. There are also small, affordable home die-cut systems for you to use.

PRINTERS AND COPIERS

Printers and copiers are magical devices for today's crafter. Take your picture and enlarge or reduce it,

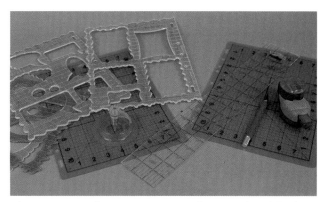
Shape cutters, rulers, compasses, craft mat and craft knife.

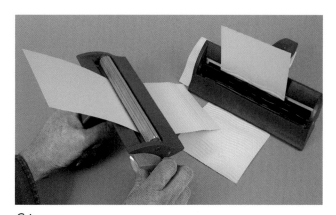
Crimpers.

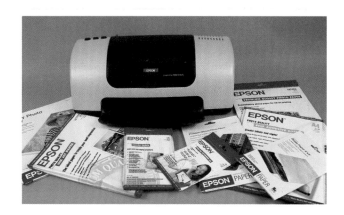
Epson Stylus Photo Ink Jet Printer and Epson specialty papers.

make mirror images, or change it from black and white to sepia tone. I love the possibilities!

I used an Epson Stylus Photo Ink Jet Printer for many of the projects within this book. Epson also has many specialty papers and products for the printer. Look down the aisles of your office supply store and see all the different ways you can use your printer or copier. Don't forget to look for those specialty papers, too.

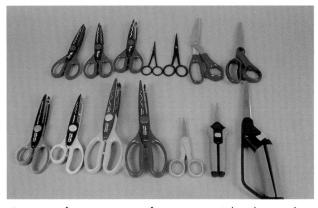

An assortment of punches.

An array of scissors—some for cutting straight edges and others for creating decorative edges.

Stencils.

PUNCH AIDS

Several of the projects in this book use hundreds of a single punch. A punch aide makes punching go faster, and it is easier on the hands. I used Power Punch by Tapestry in Time. It has changeable plates that fit most of my punches.

PUNCHES

Punches are the smallest die-cut machines! They come in various handheld and tabletop styles. There are border punches and punches that can reach further across the page.

Larger, simpler punches are the workhorses of the punches. They can punch cardstock, sometimes even several layers at a time.

The more complex and smaller punches, such as corner punches, are best used with thinner papers.

RULERS AND COMPASSES

Clear acrylic rulers with grids are very useful for measuring and positioning. Most are also compatible with craft knives and are sturdy enough to hold the blade in place during cutting.

SCISSORS

Good straight scissors are a must for any serious crafter. Cutting a crisp, clean edge is very important. Small scissors are perfect for detail cutting. Decorative edged scissors come in a range of mini to jumbo designs. The designs also go from a simple deckle to Victorian. Choose the design that suits your project. Each pair of decorative edge scissors has two designs. When you cut a test piece of paper remember what side of the cut you want to use for your project. Each side is a different design.

SHAPE CUTTERS

There are several companies that manufacture shape cutters in ovals, circles, and even rectangles. Be sure to use a self-healing mat on your cutting surface and a sharp blade for the best results. Practice makes perfect, so make sure to practice on regular paper before you cut into your decorative papers or special photos.

STENCILS

There are stencils for letters, shapes, paper dolls, and more. These come in handy if you are matching sizes, especially in clothes for paper dolls or lettering for a page.

CHAPTER 2 MATERIALS

ADHESIVES

Adhesives come in several forms and have different purposes. They are first divided into temporary and permanent. Temporary adhesives can be repositioned. I have designated which type should be used in each project.

Below are listed the various types of adhesives and their advantages and disadvantages. You choose which ones are best suited to your needs.

Aleene's® Platinum Bond™ Glass and Bead Adhesive by Duncan Enterprises
This adhesive is great for use on glass. It also works well for beads, ceramics, hard plastics, and jewelry.

Aleene's® Quick Dry Tacky Glue® by Duncan Enterprises
Tacky glue is great for adhering small pieces to your project.

E-6000 Industrial Strength Multi-Purpose Adhesive by Eclectic Products
This is a strong glue to use with glass and beads, plastics, and mirrors.

Foam Squares and Dots
These items are about ⅛" high with double-sided adhesive. They are used to give dimension to your projects and can be stacked for more height.

Keep A Memory™ by ThermOWeb
This is a temporary adhesive that comes in sheets and tapes. It is punch-friendly.

Peel n Stick™ by ThermOWeb
Peel n Stick is a double-sided permanent adhesive. I don't like putting this adhesive on paper that will be punched because it gums up the punch, but I do use Peel n Stick on projects that are cut with scissors and need the extra-strength adhesive.

Sticky Dots™ by ThermOWeb
This product can be applied to shapes after they have been punched and is a temporary adhesive.

Xyron
The Xyron machine comes in several sizes and uses adhesive cartridges. These cartridges can be temporary or permanent.

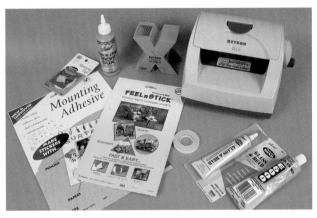

Various types of adhesives.

EYELETS

Metal eyelets are available in various sizes and colors and can be applied to anything. Holes for eyelets are punched with a hole punch to match the size of the eyelet. Eyelet setters are used to finish off and secure an eyelet.

FINISHES

Decoupage Medium
This medium is used to seal applied papers to a surface. I used decoupage medium in many projects to submerge papers and even out the surface of the project. Decoupage medium should be followed by varnish to add durability to the project. It is available in satin or gloss finishes. Decoupage medium is available in craft stores in an 8-ounce container.

Kreative Kanvas II® by Kunin Felt
This is a precoated surface that needs no preparation or hemming. It is durable and easy to work on, and I have used it for all the floor cloth projects. It is available in precut sizes or in yardage.

Paints
I used acrylic paint on all of the projects painted in this book.

Polyurethane Varnish
This is a tough finish that seals a surface. Choose either satin or gloss finish.

Spray Varnish
Spray is recommended for projects that include markers or pens. Spray many light coats so that the project can be sealed without the color running.

LUGGAGE AND KEY TAGS

These metal rings can be purchased at your local office supply store. Look at the different sizes and colors available.

PAPERS

Papers usually come in one of two sizes: 8½" x 11" or 12" x 12". There are larger sheets of specialty papers.

Many types of paper can go through your printer.

Metallics, animal prints, leather-look, and other faux finishes are a few of the textured papers available. Just looking at the varieties of textures and finishes that are available should keep you in ideas for a long time!

Luggage and key tags, as well as a few examples of precut die-cuts.

Above: Textured papers can come in metallic, animal prints, leather-looks, and other faux finishes.

At right: A seemingly endless supply of decorative and printed papers.

Cardstock

Cardstock comes in several weights and every color under the sun. It is available in both standard sizes. Cardstock is used when you need a little more weight or stability in your project.

Corrugated Papers

The corrugation can be straight or wavy. This paper type comes in many colors.

Decorative or Print Papers

Prints come in both standard sizes, and some are two-sided. There are a variety of all-over print papers and bordered designs available. Look at the wide selection of themes and coordinating prints and solids.

Handmade Papers

These specialty papers come in many sizes and textures. I used the large sizes to make the pillows in this book.

Paper Wood

This is real wood cut into paper-thin sheets. Think of the possibilities! Paper wood can be punched, cut, and run though your printer.

Vellums

Translucent papers come in white and a variety of colors. Some are adhesive-backed. Vellum will go through your printer.

PENS

Use any of your scrapbooking markers for home décor projects. If you are using them on painted furniture or floor cloths, be sure to seal the item with many light coats of spray varnish. After sealing the pen colors, you may use decoupage medium and then finish it off with varnish.

PHOTOS

You can decoupage photos or use a photocopy if you don't want to use the original. Out of focus or multiple-shot photos can be used for photo mosaic projects. Cut the photos into stone- or tile-size squares. Look at the Photo Mosaic Fire Screen Box (page 26) or Mosaic Box (page 76) for just two possibilities.

PRECUT DIE-CUTS

Many shops carry a variety of die-cut shapes already cut for you. Packages of die-cuts can include all of the same shape or a collection of shapes with theme (like back to school, camping, beach, and more).

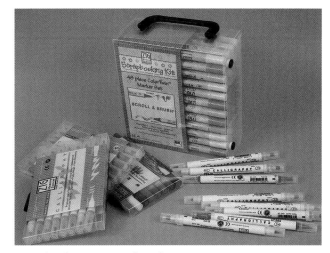

Scrapbooking pens and markers.

Assorted glossy and matte finish photos in rock colors such as browns, black, white, and beige are used in the Photo Mosaic Fire Screen project, shown above.

Die-cut hearts.

PRINTABLE FABRICS

You can put these fabrics through your printer. There are two variations of printable fabrics. One can be fused to, and the other is sewn onto, your projects. There are also photo transfer products that can be used to transfer a photo onto your fabric.

STICKERS

Stickers come in all sizes and subjects. Some have individual designs, while others come in groupings. Laser cut lace look and border stickers were used on the Room Divider (page 86).

Letter stickers come in different colors and sizes, too.

WALLPAPER PASTE

Wallpaper paste was used with paper towel pieces to cover several projects. This gives the project a papier-mâché-like surface. You can purchase this item premixed or in powder form ready to be mixed with water. If using the powder form, be sure to follow the package instructions to avoid lumps.

Sheets of paper wood on top of a piece of printable fabric.

Examples of pillows made by using a favorite photo scanned into your computer and then printed onto printable fabrics.

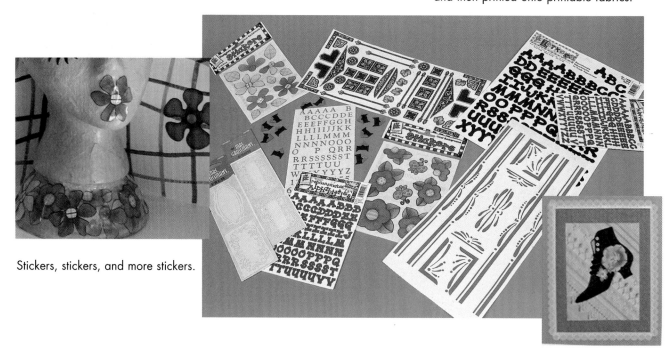

Stickers, stickers, and more stickers.

CHAPTER 3 TECHNIQUES

DECOUPAGE

MACHINE SEWING ON PAPER

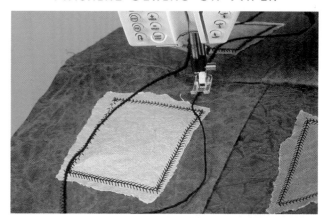

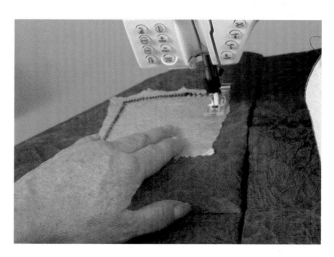

Yes, decoupage is a material, but it's a technique, too, and it's one used throughout this book, including on the Black-and-Brown Chair (page 22).

One way to apply your work to a surface is to use a permanent adhesive, such as the Xyron or Peel n Stick.

The second way is to apply a thin layer of tacky glue or decoupage medium to your work. Place your work on the wet surface and smooth it gently with the brush. Apply another layer of medium over the original surface while it is still wet and smooth with your paintbrush or fingers.

If you are doing decoupage on a surface that will receive a lot of wear, such as the rocker or kitchen stools, be sure to add layers of medium until the paper is submerged and the surface of the project is smooth. Always follow up with several coats of varnish to make the finish durable.

All papers that you will be sewing should first be backed with a medium- to heavy-weight fusible interfacing.

To sew, use a long stitch, such as a basting stitch, to sew all seams. Sewing with stitches that are too close together will perforate the seam and cause the paper to tear easily. The technique is shown in photos above, as used in the Four-Square Pillow (page 24).

MOTHER-OF-PEARL

Apply a sheet of double-sided adhesive (like Keep A Memory) to the back of a sheet of vellum.

Cut a sheet of aluminum foil slightly larger than the vellum. Ball up the foil and smooth it out again.

Apply the foil to the back of the vellum sheet with the shiny side towards the vellum.

Apply a thin second sheet of adhesive to the back of the aluminum foil. Do not remove the backing from the adhesive until after it has been punched or cut and you are ready to apply it to your project.

This technique is used in the Mother-of-Pearl Vase instructions (page 30), which is shown in the photos below.

PHOTO MOSAICS

Cutting photographs to represent tiles or stones is a great way to put to use your out-of-focus or unwanted photographs. All those shots that don't make it into your scrapbooks are perfect for this technique. Satin or glossy photos give different appearances to your project.

I used glossy photos for the Photo Mosaic Box (page 76) and a combination of glossy and satin photos on the Photo Mosaic Fire Screen (page 26). Photos of the technique used in both projects are shown below.

Simply cut the shapes desired out of photographs you would otherwise not use.

PUNCH TECHNIQUES

There are so many shapes and sizes of punches. They are sturdy little machines, if you use them with care and for what they are designed to do. A general rule for what to punch with each is: the more intricate the design on the punch, the lighter the weight of the paper to be punched. If you have to stand on the punch to make it work, you are punching the wrong material. This will surely destroy the alignment of your punch, and it will break.

Never use permanent adhesive, such as Peel n Stick, on the paper to be punched. The first few punches will work, but then a build-up of the adhesive will occur and the punch will start to stick when you use it later. If you need to use permanent adhesive on the back of a punch, put the punched shape through the Xyron with a permanent adhesive cartridge installed.

Keep A Memory double-sided adhesive is a temporary adhesive and has not hurt my punches. It gives a great bond for paper on most surfaces.

Corner Punches

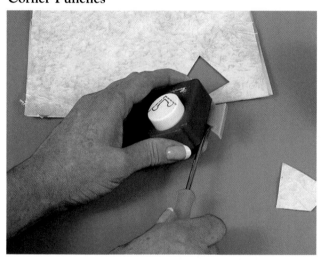

Corner punches are unique in that they are equipped with guides that only allow the corner of the paper into the punch.

Three guides can be wiggled out with a screwdriver. This does not hurt the guides, which fit together like puzzle pieces and can come in and out as desired. When the guides are removed, the corner punch can be used to punch a decorative border along a sheet of paper. Several of the projects in this book use this technique.

To line up a series of punches, position the punch upside-down so that you can see where you are punching. This helps to align the design across a page.

Border Punches

Border punches go along the edge of your paper.

If you want a continuous border, use the punch upside-down so you can align it properly with the previous punch.

Border punches work best on thin paper.

SEALING PHOTOCOPIES AND INKS

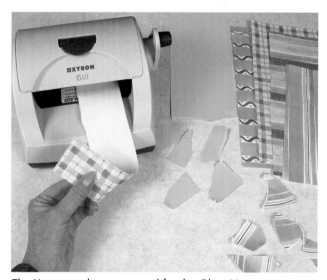

The Xyron machine was used for the Glass Vase project (page 123), but a little differently than usual. You can see above that the paper went through print side down so the adhesive was on the print side for placement on the inside of the vase. Generally, you would place the paper through print side up for adhesive on the back of your paper.

Spray light coats of sealer over scanned photos from ink jet printers. This will prevent the ink from bleeding when the decoupage medium is applied.

This method also works where scrapbooking color pens have been used. First seal the surface with several light coats of varnish, and then add decoupage medium.

CHAPTER 4 ◆

PROJECTS FOR YOUR DEN

What colors better to work with than neutrals?

For the den, I wanted items of interest—things that would spark the décor of a large room but not overpower it.

Within the projects in this chapter, you'll find I've invented a few new techniques that really fool the eye! Aluminum foil and vellum can be used together to make faux mother-of-pearl, for example. I used this technique on vases, but it can be used on any surface with any punch you own.

Another great look is the photo mosaic. It uses all those "oops" photos that normally get thrown away. Don't we all have a drawer full of those?

And sewing on paper to create pillows is a great technique that can add real panache to your sofa.

So choose your neutrals and add a few punches of color—maybe a metallic or two—and you'll have a transformed den in no time!

Decorative Balls with Punched Designs ◆

MATERIALS

6 3½" papier-mâché balls by DCC
DecoArt™ Americana® Acrylic Paint
- 2 oz. bottle Buttermilk
- 2 oz. bottle Russet

Emagination Crafts, Inc.™
Craft Punches
- Circle (small)
- Ivy Leaf (large)
- Holly Leaf (large)
- Rabbit (large)
- Teardrop (large)
- Oval (large)
- Hawthorne Leaf (jumbo)
- Ivy Leaf (jumbo)
- Dusty Miller Leaf (jumbo)
- Grapevine Leaf (jumbo)
- Contemporary Tree (jumbo)
- Allegro (jumbo)

Emagination Crafts, Inc.™
Bravissimo! Paper™ (8½" x 11")
- 1 sheet Safari Leopard
- 1 sheet Patina Gold-Gold Mine
- 1 sheet Affluent
- 1 sheet Fire Ice-Line
- 1 sheet Sumptuous
- 1 sheet Citrine-Swirl
- 1 sheet Metallic Gold-Pure Diamond

8 oz. container gloss decoupage medium
Tacky glue
Paintbrush

INSTRUCTIONS

1 Paint three balls with Buttermilk acrylic paint.
2 Paint the other three with Russet acrylic. Let dry completely.

For Ball 1:
1 Select a ball painted with Buttermilk paint.
2 Punch approximately 40 Hawthorne leaves from Safari Leopard paper.
3 Cut the stem off of each leaf.
4 Glue leaves on the ball starting at the top. Using Figure 1 as a guide, leave space between leaves and vary position of each leaf so that each one faces a different direction.

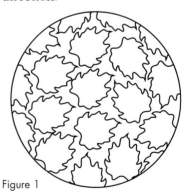

Figure 1

For Ball 2:
1 Select a ball painted with Buttermilk paint.
2 Cover the ball with jumbo and large ivy leaf punches from Patina Gold-Gold Mine paper.
3 Arrange the ivy in vines as shown in Figure 2.

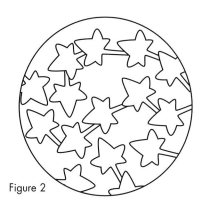

Figure 2

For Ball 3:

1 Select a ball painted with Buttermilk paint.

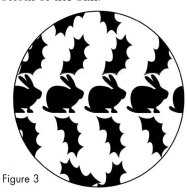

2 Using Affluent paper, punch 13 rabbits.

3 Glue the rabbits around the circumference of the ball with all of them facing the same direction. Follow the pattern shown on Figure 3. Figure 4 shows the pattern as viewed from the top or bottom of the ball.

Figure 3

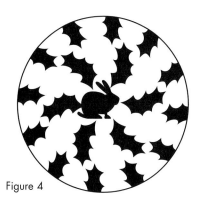

Figure 4

For Ball 4:

1 Select a ball painted with Russet paint.

2 Punch 15 grapevine leaves from Fire Ice-Line paper.

3 Punch 17 ovals and eight small circles from Patina Gold-Gold Mine paper.

4 Around the circumference of the ball, arrange five grapevine leaves with five ovals between the leaves, as shown in Figure 5. Figure 6 shows the pattern as viewed from the top or bottom of the ball.

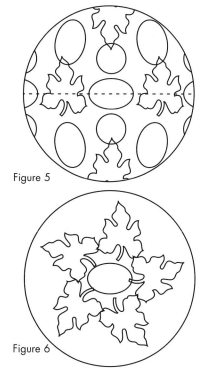

Figure 5

Figure 6

For Ball 5:

1 Select a ball painted with Russet paint.

2 Punch two small circles and 20 teardrops from Metallic Gold-Pure Diamond paper.

3 Glue the circle on the bottom of the ball.

4 Glue the 10 teardrops around the circle as shown in Figure 7. Repeat the same pattern on the top of the ball.

5 Then, punch 30 Dusty Miller leaves from Citrine-Swirl paper and 40 teardrops from Metallic Gold-Pure Diamond paper. See Figure 8 for placement.

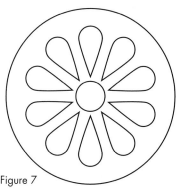

Figure 7

Figure 8

For Ball 6:

1 Select a ball painted with Russet paint.

2 Using Sumptuous paper, punch 18 small circles, 16 Allegro punches, and 12 tree punches.

3 See Figure 9 for punches and placement.

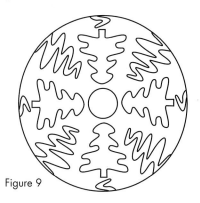

Figure 9

Black, Silver, and Cardboard Mirror ◆

MATERIALS

Unfinished 18" square wooden framed
  mirror
DecoArt™ Americana® Satins
  Acrylic Enamel
  • 8 oz. jar Black Satin
8 oz. can DecoArt™ Americana®
  Polyurethane Varnish
2 sheets Kraft Wavy Corrugated Paper
  by DMD Paper Reflections®
  (8½" x 11")
Emagination Crafts, Inc.™
  Craft Punches
  • Quilt Square (super giant)
  • Quilt Square (super jumbo)
Emagination Crafts, Inc.™
  Bravissimo! Paper (8½" x 11")
  • 2 sheets King (silver metallic)
Tacky glue
Permanent adhesive
Paintbrush

INSTRUCTIONS

1 Paint the wooden frame with Black Satin paint, and let dry.

2 Punch 26 kraft super giant squares and cut in half diagonally.
3 Use glue to apply the triangles to the mirror frame. Two triangles at the inside corners will need to be trimmed to fit corner.
4 Using the King paper, punch four silver super giant squares and 20 super jumbo squares.

5 Center the four super giant King squares in each corner black rectangle and glue so that the silver square is framed by black.
6 Glue super jumbo silver squares so they are framed by black.

7 Apply several coats of varnish to the completed frame.

◆Black-and-Brown Table

MATERIALS

Any size table
 (This one is 15" x 15" x 30".)
DecoArt™ Americana® Satins
 Acrylic Enamel
 • 8 oz. jar Black Satin
8 oz. can DecoArt™ Americana®
 Polyurethane Varnish
Emagination Crafts, Inc.™
 Craft Punches
 • Oval (super giant)
 • Quilt Diamond – 60º (super jumbo)
 • Circle (small)
1 sheet heavy-weight kraft paper
 (30" square)
Permanent adhesive
Paintbrush

INSTRUCTIONS

1 Paint the legs black. Let dry.

2 Punch four ovals and apply them with the permanent adhesive to the center face of each side of the table.

3 Next, punch eight diamonds and apply one on each side of every oval.

4 Punch eight small circles and apply them to the outside of each diamond. The pattern on each side of the table should be as follows: circle, diamond, oval, diamond, circle.

5 Cut eight wavy strips of kraft paper approximately the length of the legs and ½" wide.

6 Apply the strips down the front side of each leg.

7 Apply several coats of varnish to the entire table.

Note: If your table does not have a natural wood-grain top as ours did, you may also want to paint the top black and decorate with punches as well.

Black-and-Brown Chair ◆

Flea market-type chair (Note: Select a chair with a wooden seat and adjust the design to fit your chair. I used these instructions specifically to fit the chair I selected.)

DecoArt™ Americana® Satins Acrylic Enamel
- 8 oz. jar Black Satin

8 oz. can DecoArt™ Americana® Polyurethane Varnish

Emagination Crafts, Inc.™ Craft Punches
- Chevron (super giant)
- Circle (super jumbo)
- Quilt Square (super jumbo)
- Quilt Diamond – 60º (super jumbo)
- Quilt Triangle (jumbo)

Emagination Crafts, Inc.™ Bravissimo! Papers (8½" x 11")
- 1 sheet Patina Copper
- 1 sheet Patina Gold
- 1 sheet Gold Mine
- 1 sheet King (metallic silver)

1 sheet Silver Daler Canford Paper (8½" x 11")

8 oz. container gloss decoupage medium

Ruler

Scissors

Paintbrush

INSTRUCTIONS

1 Paint the chair black. Let dry.

2 Punch 14 super jumbo circles from Gold Mine paper.

3 Cut circles in half.

4 Decoupage the half-circles around the edge of the chair seat, with the flat edge of the punches against the outside edge of the seat and the rounded edges of the punches pointing toward the seat center.

5 Punch 26 quilt triangles from Daler Canford Silver paper.

6 Decoupage the quilt triangles between the half-circles, with the center point of the triangle pointing toward the outside edge of the seat.

7 Using the ruler and scissors, cut a 6" square from Patina Gold paper.

8 Decoupage the square to the center of the seat to form a diamond.

9 Cut Swirl Pattern, shown below, out of King paper, and apply it to the center of the diamond.

10 Punch 12 chevrons from Patina Copper and 12 more from Patina Gold.

11 Apply to the chair back in two rows, alternating the two colors and with the chevron point facing up.

12 Punch three diamonds from King paper and use them to accent the chair back. Center one on each side and one on the seat of the chair.

13 Punch four diamonds from King paper and one from Patina Gold.

14 Decoupage one diamond on each front leg of the chair.

15 Decoupage two King diamonds on either side of a Patina Gold diamond on the center of the rung below the chair seat.

16 Finish by applying several coats of varnish. Be sure to let dry between coats.

Black and Brown Chair Swirl Pattern

Four-Square Pillow ◆

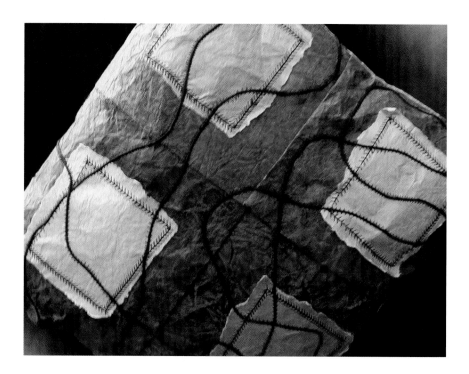

Emagination Crafts, Inc.™ Handmade
 Indian Paper (8½" x 11")
 • 2 sheets Burgundy Leather
 • 2 sheets Brown Leather
 • 2 sheets Copper
 • 2 sheets Gold
1 skein Emagination Crafts, Inc.™
 Variegated Ebony Twist Art®
 Paper Yarn
14" x 14" Pop In Pillow® Pillow Insert
 by Fairfield
Black sewing thread
1 yard fusible interfacing
18" x 18" brown kraft paper
Hot glue gun and glue sticks
12 clothespins
Iron
Sewing machine

INSTRUCTIONS

1 Back the Burgundy Leather and Brown Leather papers with fusible interfacing.

2 Take the kraft paper and squish it into a ball several times to soften up the paper. After the paper is soft and pliable, iron on the interfacing.

3 Place right sides together of one Burgundy Leather paper and one Brown Leather paper and sew long basting stitches down one 11" side. Do the same thing with the second set of leather papers. See Figure 1 for design details.

Burgundy	Brown
Brown	Burgundy

Figure 1

4 Finger-press the seams to one side.

5 With right sides together, match a burgundy square to a brown square. Sew together.

6 Tear two Gold squares and two Copper papers into approximately 4" squares.

7 Use a decorative stitch to sew them on top of the brown and burgundy papers.

8 Use a zigzag stitch to couch the twist art yarn in a freeform pattern over the front squares.

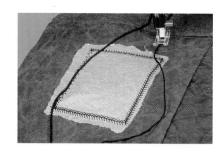

9 With right sides together, sew three sides together. Trim seams and corners.

10 Turn right-side out and insert pillow form.

11 Fold the seam of the open side in towards the pillow and glue together. Use clothespins to hold the seam while drying.

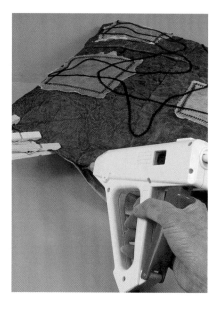

◆Black Pillow with Dots and Eyelets

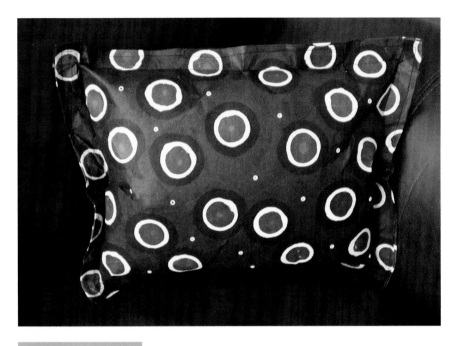

MATERIALS

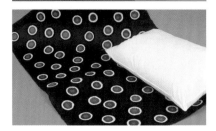

22" x 31" sheet Handmade Paper
by Lacey Paper Co.
12" x16" Soft 'n' Crafty Pillow Form
by Fairfield
Approximately 20 Emagination Crafts,
Inc.™ ivory eyelets
Emagination Crafts, Inc.™ Eyelet Setter
Emagination Crafts, Inc.™ Craft Punch
• ½" hole punch
Black sewing thread
Sewing machine
22" x 30" fusible interfacing
Iron

INSTRUCTIONS

1 Cut handmade paper in half to form two pieces that measure 22" x 15½".
2 Cut interfacing a little larger and apply to back side of each piece of paper.

3 Trim interfacing to size.
4 Punch holes for eyelets over the 12" x 16" center of the pillow top.
5 Add eyelets, as shown in the next three photos.

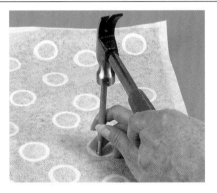

6 With wrong sides together, sew around three sides of the papers.
7 Insert pillow form and sew across open side.

8 Fold in raw edges all around the pillow.
9 Leave a 1" flange and topstitch around the outside edges.

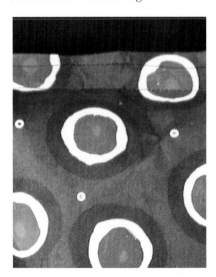

Photo Mosaic Fire Screen ◆

MATERIALS

Plywood
- 1 piece 31" x 28"
- 2 pieces 31" x 10"

4 1" hinges

DecoArt™ Americana® Satins Acrylic Enamel
- 8 oz. jar Black Satin
- 8 oz. jar Dark Ecru

Sea sponge

1"-wide painters' tape

Assorted photos (Glossy and matte finish in rock colors: browns, black, white, beige, etc.; you will need approximately 60 light "stones" on each side panel and 200 light stones in the center, approximately 100 assorted dark stones for design on center panel, and approximately 50 assorted dark for each side panel.)

Tacky glue

Paper plate

Scissors

Paintbrush

INSTRUCTIONS

1 Connect hinges to plywood with the large piece in the center.

2 Paint all sides and edges of plywood with Black Satin paint. Let dry completely.

3 Lay fire screen on a flat surface and tape off 1" border around edges of each piece of plywood.

4 Pour Dark Ecru satin paint into a paper plate and dab sea sponge into paint. Pounce the sponge over the surface of the screen. Cover most of the surface, giving it the look of cement.

5 Remove the tape to reveal a 1" black border around each section of the screen. Let dry completely.

6 Cut approximately 200 dark stone shapes out of the photos.

7 Arrange stones on the screen as shown in the illustration below.

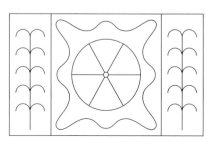

8 Cut approximately 320 lighter-colored stone shapes and use them to fill in the background, as shown in the photo below.

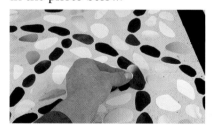

You can leave the surface of the fire screen in this state, or you can apply several coats of polyurethane.

Safety tip: Use the screen in front of the fireplace only when there is no fire lit inside.

◆ Black-and-Brown Floor Cloth

INSTRUCTIONS

1 Paint floor cloth with Black Satin paint and let dry.

2 Mark off a 3" border on the short ends of the cloth with painters' tape.

3 Use a rotary cutter to cut all three colors of cardstock into assorted-width strips from ⅜" to ½" wide.

4 Cut the strips into 3" sections. Enough 3" strips are needed to fill the border edge and give the impression of fringe.

5 Adhere the strips to the marked off border, making the top edge straight across. Leave black showing between cardstock strips.

6 Mark off a ⅜" line of black on each side before adhering the next border.

7 Punch 42 super giant quilt squares from the Silver Metallic paper and cut them in half diagonally to create 84 triangles.

Continued on next page

MATERIALS

36" x 24" Kreative Kanvas II® precoated surface by Kunin Felt
DecoArt™ Americana® Satins Acrylic Enamel
• 8 oz. jar Black Satin
8 oz. can DecoArt™ Americana® Polyurethane Varnish
Emagination Crafts, Inc.™ Craft Punches
• Circles (small, large, super giant, and super jumbo)
• Quilt Square (super giant)
Fiskars® Rotary Paper Edger (45mm Rotary Wave Blade)
4 sheets Silver Metallic Daler Canford Paper (8½" x 11")
Cardstock by DMD Paper Reflections® (8½" x 11")
• 1 sheet Stone (light)
• 6 sheets Ginger (medium)
• 2 sheets Buckeye (dark)
Permanent adhesive
1"-wide painters' tape
Rotary cutter
Circle template or die-cut (optional)
Scissors
Paintbrush

8 Evenly space the triangles in a border all around the floor cloth, leaving ⅛" between the floor cloth edge and each triangle as well as ⅛" between each triangle, as shown below.

9 Cut approximately 30 4" Ginger circles. (Use a circle template or a die-cut if possible.)

10 Punch a super jumbo hole in each Ginger circle. Save the punch-outs.

11 Adhere the Ginger circles irregularly over the cloth, as shown in the placement diagram below.

12 Punch 30 large circles from Buckeye paper and adhere on top of each Ginger circle.

13 Punch a large hole in each of the super jumbo Ginger punch-outs saved from step 10 and

adhere them on the cloth to fill around the 4" Ginger circles.

14 Punch small Stone circles and adhere one on each super jumbo Ginger punch-out, as shown here.

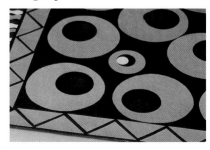

15 Apply many light coats of varnish.

Black-and-Brown Floor Cloth Punch Placement Diagram

◆ Silver Punched Vase

MATERIALS

9" x 7½" short-neck papier-mâché vase
  by DCC
Emagination Crafts, Inc.™
  Craft Punches
  • Impatien Leaf (large and jumbo)
DecoArt™ Dazzling Metallics
  Acrylic Paint
  • 4 oz. bottle Shimmering Silver
  • 4 oz. bottle Pewter
The Ultimate! Glue™ by Crafters' Pick
Papers by Catherine (8½" x 11")
  • 5 sheets Silver
  • 5 sheets Graphite
Paintbrush

INSTRUCTIONS

1 Paint the top half and inside of the vase with Shimmering Silver paint and let dry.

2 Paint the bottom half and bottom with Pewter paint. Let dry completely.

3 Punch 264 jumbo leaves from Silver paper and 264 large leaves from the Graphite paper.

4 Glue each Graphite leaf on top of a Silver leaf. Line up the bottom stems of the leaves, as shown in Figure 1.

Figure 1

5 Begin gluing a row of 22 leaf sets approximately 2½" from the bottom of the vase. Glue the leaf sets with pointed end down and as close as possible to each other.

6 The second row begins halfway up the leaves and over the point at which they meet, as shown in Figure 2.

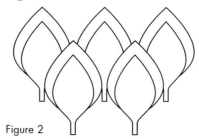

Figure 2

7 Continue gluing the rows to the neck of the vase, about 12 rows total to complete the look.

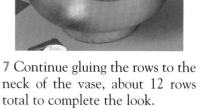

Mother-of-Pearl Vase ◆━━━━━━━━

MATERIALS

11½" x 9" papier-mâché vase by DCC
DecoArt™ Americana® Acrylic Paint
  • 4 oz. bottle Black
Emagination Crafts, Inc.™ The Edge™
  Scissors (scalloped)
Emagination Crafts, Inc.™ Craft Punches
  • Quilt Kite (super giant)
  • Oval (super giant)
  • Quilt Diamond – 45° (super jumbo)
  • Mounties™ – Snidely
  • Circle (large)
  • Quasar (small and ribbon)
Emagination Crafts, Inc.™
  Bravissimo! Paper™ (8½" x 11")
  • 2 sheets King (silver metallic)
Vellum by DMD Paper Reflections®
  (8½" x 11")
  • 2 sheets White Cloud
  • 1 sheet Bordeaux (medium brown)
8 sheets Keep A Memory™ double-sided
  adhesive from ThermOWeb
  (8½" x 11")
3 sheets heavy-duty aluminum foil
  (9½" x 13")
8 oz. jar gloss decoupage medium
Paintbrush

INSTRUCTIONS

1 Paint the vase black on both the inside and outside. Let dry completely

2 Cover the paint with two coats of gloss decoupage medium. Let dry between coats.

3 Begin the mother-of-pearl process by applying a sheet of double-sided adhesive to the back of each piece of White Cloud and Bordeaux vellum.

4 Crinkle foil, smooth it out again, and apply it with double-sided adhesive to the back of all three vellum pieces, making sure the shiny side of the foil is towards the vellum.

5 Apply a second sheet of double-sided adhesive to the back of the foil. However, do not remove the paper backing from the second sheet of adhesive until you are ready to apply it to the vase.

6 Add adhesive to the back of the two King metallic sheets.

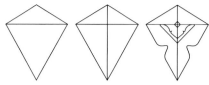

Figure 1

7 Referring to Figure 1, which shows how each punch is used on the kite punch, punch approximately 18 quilt diamonds from prepared White Cloud vellum.

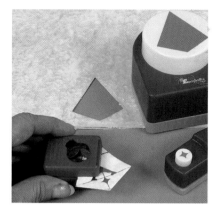

8 Remove the paper backing from the punches and apply to the vase, following Punch Placement illustration, page 32, as a guide.
9 Use the scallop scissors to cut nine ½" x 9" strips from the prepared Bordeaux vellum and apply with double-sided adhesive to the vase, again referring to Punch Placement for placement instruction.
10 Punch 27 quilt diamonds from King paper and apply 18 around the neck edge of the vase so that

approximately two-thirds of the diamond is on the outside of the vase and one-third is applied inside the opening. See Punch Placement for details.
11 Place two diamonds on each insert with the scalloped strip of Bordeux between them.
12 Punch 18 small quasars from prepared Bordeaux vellum and refer to Punch Placement for placement details.

13 Coat the vase with two coats of gloss decoupage medium.

Tip: The design made by the Mounties punch in Figure 1 above is achieved after removing the corner guides installed on the punch, as shown in the photos at right.

They can be removed temporarily without creating damage to the punch.

Pry them loose with a slotted screwdriver as shown and replace when punching is finished.

Note: The Punch Placement illustration, page 32, shows which paper is used and where all of the punches are placed on the vase.

The section with the strip of the brown scalloped strip is used in repeats around the vase nine times.

The strips with the oval repeat nine times around the vase.

The 18 diamonds at the top of the vase go over the top edge of the vase. The diamonds at the bottom of the scalloped strips go under the bottom of the vase.

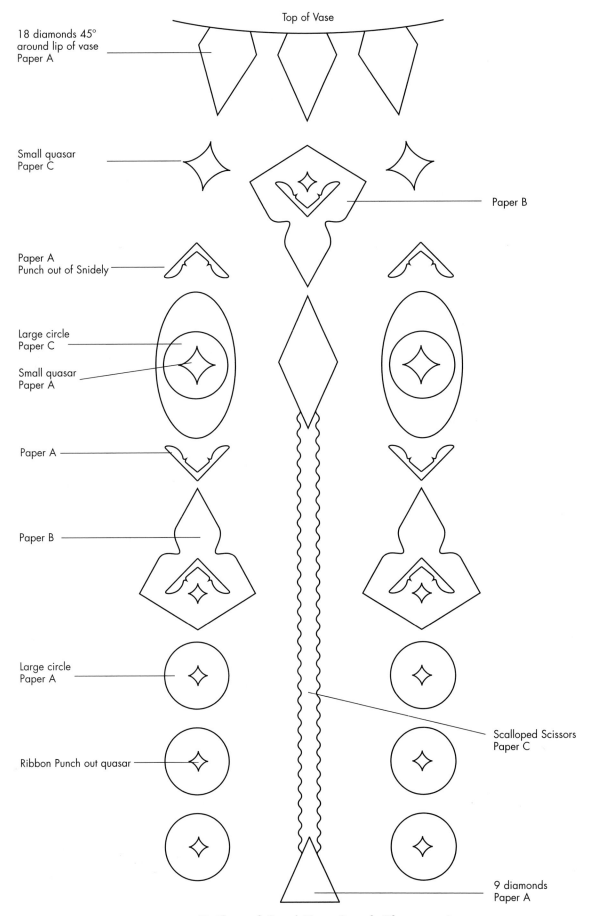

18 diamonds 45°
around lip of vase
Paper A

Top of Vase

Small quasar
Paper C

Paper B

Paper A
Punch out of Snidely

Large circle
Paper C

Small quasar
Paper A

Paper A

Paper B

Large circle
Paper A

Scalloped Scissors
Paper C

Ribbon Punch out quasar

9 diamonds
Paper A

Mother-of-Pearl Vase Punch Placement

The possibilities for different vase designs are seemingly endless. Here are several ideas for other types of vases you might want to try. Each follows steps similar to the Mother-of-Pearl Vase. Only the Black Vase with Mother-of-Pearl Inlay requires use of foil to replicate the mother-of-pearl look. For the other vases, you may skip steps 3 through 5 in the Mother-of-Pearl Vase. Listed under each photograph below are the materials necessary to re-create each look.

Black Vase with Mother-of-Pearl Inlay

Use 9" x 7½" short-neck papier-mâché vase by DCC, DecoArt™ Americana® Satins Lamp Black acrylic enamel, and DecoArt™ Dazzling Metallics® Bronze acrylic paint. Emagination Crafts Punches: Oak Leaf (small), Circle (small), Triangle (small), Flower (large), Butterfly (large), White Oak Leaf (jumbo), and Grapevine Leaf (jumbo). The Edge Decorative-Edged Scissors: Scallop and Wave. Paper Reflections Vellum: White Marble (2 sheets, 8½" x 11") and Bordeaux (1 sheet, 8½" x 11"). Keep A Memory™ Mounting Adhesive by ThermOWeb (6 sheets, 8½" x 11") and heavy-duty aluminum foil (3 sheets, 8½" x 11").

Red Vase with Cream-and-Black Designs

Use 14"-tall Papier-Mâché Longneck Vase by DCC, DecoArt™ Americana® Satins True Red acrylic paint, double-sided adhesive, and DecoArt™ Americana® Polyurethane Gloss Varnish. Emagination Crafts Guardian Angel (super giant) punch. Paper Reflections Handmade Paper: Gold Florentine (3 sheets, 8½" x 11") and Black and Gold Lattice (2 sheets, 8½" x 11").

Black Vase with Silver Angels Around Throat

Use 14"-tall Papier-Mâché Longneck Vase by DCC, DecoArt™ Americana® Satins Black Satin acrylic paint, double-sided adhesive, and DecoArt™ Americana® Polyurethane Gloss Varnish. Emagination Crafts Guardian Angel (super giant) punch. Bravissimo! Paper™: King (1 sheet, 8½" x 11").

Punched Lampshade ◆━━━━━

MATERIALS

White lampshade (4" diameter at top,
   10" diameter at bottom, and 7" high)
Emagination Crafts, Inc.™
   Craft Punches
   • Quilt Hexagon (super jumbo)
   • Quilt Triangle (jumbo)
   • Circle (small and large)
   • ½" Circle (ribbon)
   • ¹⁄₁₆" Circle (ribbon)
   • Quazar (ribbon)
Emagination Crafts, Inc.™
   Bravissimo! Papers™ (8½" x 11")
   • 4 sheets Patina Copper
   • 1 sheet King (silver metallic)
   • 1 sheet Patina Green
1 sheet Terra Cotta Vellum by DMD
   Paper Reflections (8½" x 11")
6 sheets Keep A Memory™ double-sided
   adhesive by ThermOWeb™
   (8½" x 11")
2 sheets heavy-weight white paper
   (18" x 24")
Tacky glue
Cutting mat
8½" x 11" piece of ½"-thick foam
   (Styrofoam, packing foam, or anything smooth and even that allows a
   piercing tool through easily.)
Piercing tool or
   a large, thick sewing needle
Pencil
Scissors or rotary tool
Light box

INSTRUCTIONS

1 Lay the lampshade on its side on top of one of the 18" x 24" white paper sheets.

2 Starting with the seam, draw along the top and the bottom of the lampshade as you roll it across the paper. Add ½" at one end for the overlap seam, ½" at the bottom of the shade, and 1" at the top edge of the shade.

3 Cut out. This is the pattern.

4 Place the pattern on the second white sheet and trace. This second white sheet will be the base of the new lampshade.

5 Fold the original pattern in half and in half again.

6 Make a pattern of the quarter section of the shade. You will be making four separate pieces for the complete shade. Each quarter section fits on one 8½" x 11" sheet

of the paper we are using to make the shade.

7 Back all four sheets of Patina Copper paper with double-sided adhesive. Trace the quarter shade pattern on each sheet and cut them out.

8 Remove the backing and attach all four panels to the front side of the shade cover. It's all right to have slight gaps between the panels. These will be covered later.

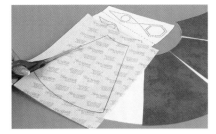

9 Trim the top and the bottom edges of the shade, if needed, to even out both edges.

10 Make four copies of the piercing pattern, which is located on the next page, and cut them out.

11 Punch the hexagons out of one. Use this pattern to mark the hexagons punch-outs on all four sections. Punch them out, as

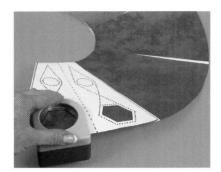

shown in the following photo.

12 Repeat procedure for triangles and circles.

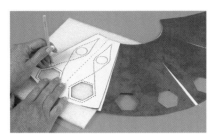

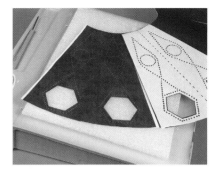

13 Pierce holes, as shown.

14 Glue vellum behind the triangles, circles, and hexagons.

It is quite simple to make variations to the lampshade. Shown here are two variations, both of which follow the same basic steps as the first lampshade, but use different punches, papers, and designs. Listed under each photo are the punches and papers used for these two variations.

Punches: Quasar (small and ribbon); Circle (small, ¼" ribbon, and large); Oval (super giant); Chevron (super giant); Quilt Square (super jumbo); Dusty Miller (jumbo); and Allegro (jumbo). Papers: Bravissimo! Patina Gold (4 sheets, 8½" x 11"); Bravissimo! King (1 sheet, 8½" x 11"); Bravissimo! Patina Green (1 sheet, 11" x 13"); and Paper Reflections Deep Yellow Vellum (1 sheet, 8½" x 11").

Punches: Quasar (small and ribbon); Circle (¼" ribbon, and large); Chevron (super giant); Quilt Diamond (super jumbo); and Quilt Triangle 60° (jumbo). Papers: Bravissimo! Patina Copper (1 sheet, 8½" x 11"); Bravissimo! King (4 sheets, 8½" x 11"); and Paper Reflections White Cloud Vellum (1 sheet, 8½" x 11"). Plus, The Edge Decorative-Edge Scissors (Zipper).

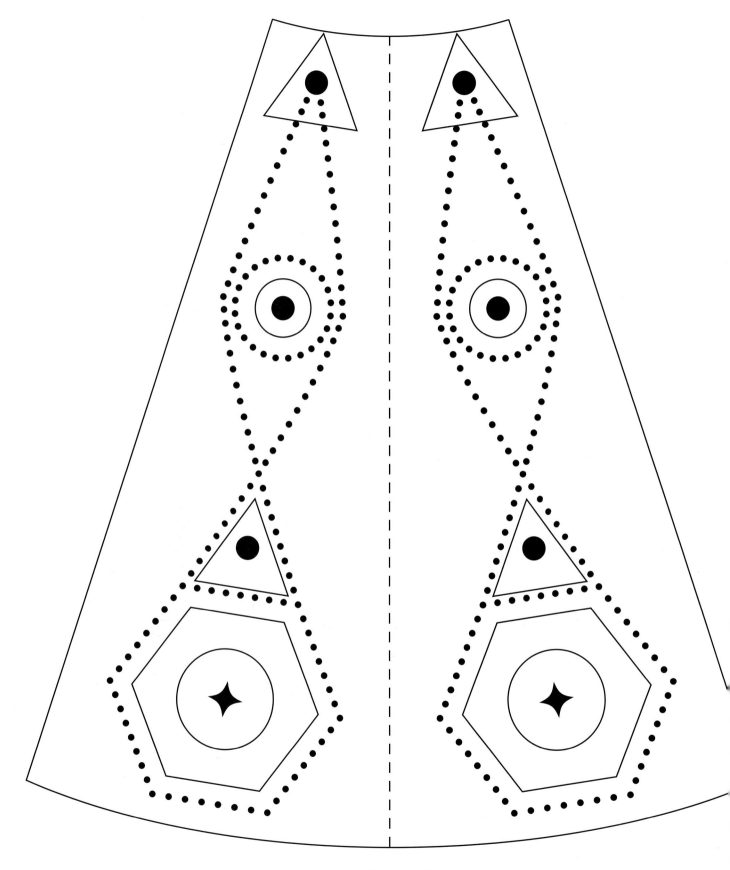

Lamp Piercing Pattern

◆ Gallery

Several other accent pieces can be designed for your den as well. Although there isn't space to detail all of the projects shown here, my hope is that seeing them will plant the seed of inspiration for you to either emulate these projects or come up with more of your own. Shown here are: grandfather clock, square wood inlay picture on framed mirror, fish box, and a silver-and-black candleholder.

CHAPTER 5 ◆

PROJECTS FOR YOUR HOME OFFICE

Simple and masculine are the words to describe the projects in this room. With the abundance of papier-mâché products available today, I was able to transform different shapes and sizes of containers into useful items.

Striving for the look of leather, but wanting it to be just a bit more exotic, I found the alligator leather-look paper and off I went. When I added the black and metallic papers for accents, I ended up with finished projects that would look great on a man's desk.

For each project, I used simple punch designs that work up quickly. The surface of the papier-mâché is sponge-painted and just a few simple punches add the finishing touches.

Any of the items in this chapter are simple enough for a beginner, but even if you're new at crafting your own home decorating projects, you'll fool everyone with these very sophisticated-looking desk accessories.

Desk Pad

MATERIALS

18" x 30" heavy mat board
   (black)
Emagination Crafts, Inc.™
   Bravissimo! Paper (8½" x 11")
   •5 sheets Tan Gator
5 sheets Black Cardstock by DMD
   Paper Reflections® (8½" x 11")
6 yards black Natural Hemp
   Cording Natural Knots™ by
   Toner Plastics
10 sheets permanent double-sided
   adhesive (8½" x 11")
⅛" hole punch
Scissors

INSTRUCTIONS

1 Cut mat board into three parts, as shown: one piece 23" x 18" for the base and two pieces 3½" x 18" for the side panels.

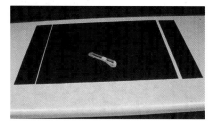

2 Adhere double-sided adhesive to one side of each piece of Tan Gator paper and black cardstock.
3 Cover the two 3½" x 18" mat board pieces with adhesive-backed Tan Gator paper. Fold under corners and then sides of the Tan Gator paper, as shown.

4 Cut two pieces of adhesive-backed black cardstock slightly smaller than the side panels (each piece should be approximately 3" x 17½") and apply to the back of each side panel.
5 Place a 2½"-wide strip of adhesive-backed black cardstock around the center of each side panel. Top these strips with 1½"-wide strips of adhesive-backed Tan Gator paper, as shown here.

6 Place side panels in position on top of the base piece.
7 Punch holes ½" in from the outside edges and approximately 1" apart the entire length of each panel, as shown in the following photo.

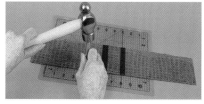

8 Cut the hemp cord in half. Dip the cut ends of the cord in glue and shape them like a needle-point. Let dry.
9 Take the sharp end of the cord and push it through the top hole on one side of the mat. Place the center of the cord in this top hole.
10 Take the top section of cord and weave it down through the second hole. Repeat this with the cord under the mat. Continue down the mat, as shown. Repeat for other side.
11 Glue the ends of the cord inside the panel.

Dome Chest

MATERIALS

4" x 6" papier-mâché dome chest
  by MB Glick
DecoArt™ Americana® Acrylic Paint
  • 2 oz. bottle Raw Sienna
8 oz. jar DecoArt™ Faux Glazing
  Medium™ Clear Art Glaze
Emagination Crafts, Inc.™
  Bravissimo! Paper (8½" x 11")
  • 2 sheets Tan Gator
DMD Paper Reflections®
  • 2 sheets Black Cardstock
    (8½" x 11")
  • 1 sheet Gold Wave Metallic
    (8½" x 5")
  • 1 sheet Copper Metallic (4" x 4")
Emagination Crafts, Inc.
  Craft Punches
  • Teardrop (large and small)
  • ¼" Circle (ribbon)
5 sheets permanent double-sided adhesive
  (8½" x 11")
Sea sponge
Tacky glue
Scissors or rotary cutter

INSTRUCTIONS

1 Mix half paint and half glazing medium together.

2 Using the sea sponge, pat the paint-glazing medium mixture over the surface of all papier-mâché pieces. Do not cover the entire surface; leave some of the original surface through to create texture, as shown below.

3 Add the double-sided adhesive to the back of all papers.

4 Cut the black cardstock into pieces to measure:
  • 4⅞" square
  • 3⅛" x 3⅝"
  • 1" x 4⅜"
  • ⅞" x 3¾"

5 Cut the Tan Gator paper to measure:
  • 4⅜" x 4⅝"
  • 1⅞" x 2¾"
  • ⅞" x 3¾"

6 On the lid, adhere pieces for the lid one layer centered on top of the other, starting with the black 4⅞" square. Center it and apply the Tan Gator 4⅜" x 4⅝" piece on top of it. Continue the layer by centering and applying the black 3⅛" x 3⅝" and finally the Tan Gator 1⅞" x 2¾", as shown below.

6 Remove the paper from the bottom piece of the layer and center and apply the layered stack to the lid of the dome chest.

7 For the front of the drawer, center and apply the ⅞" x 3¾" Tan Gator paper over the 1" x 4⅜" black cardstock piece.

8 Punch a small circle in the center of the stack through both pieces for the knob to be inserted. Adhere the stack to the center of the front face of the chest, as shown below.

9 Punch two small copper teardrops, two large gold teardrops, and one ¼" gold ribbon circle and apply to the front of the chest as shown in Figure 1.

Figure 1

Notepad Box ◆ ━━━━━━━━━

MATERIALS

Papier-mâché notepad box by MB Glick
DecoArt™ Americana® Acrylic Paint
- 2 oz. bottle Raw Sienna
8 oz. jar DecoArt™ Faux Glazing
  Medium™ Clear Art Glaze
Emagination Crafts, Inc.™
  Bravissimo! Paper (8½" x 11")
- 1 sheet Tan Gator
DMD Paper Reflections®
- 1 sheet Black Cardstock
  (8½" x 11")
- 1 sheet Gold Wave Metallic
  (8½" x 5")
- 1 sheet Copper Metallic (4" x 4")
Emagination Crafts, Inc.™
  Craft Punches
- Teardrop (large and small)
- ½" Circle (ribbon)
3 sheets permanent double-sided
  adhesive (8½" x 11")
Sea sponge
Tacky glue
Scissors or rotary cutter

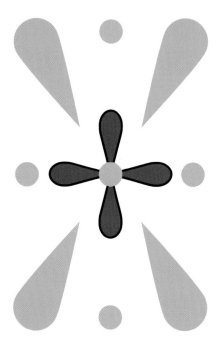

INSTRUCTIONS

1 Sponge paint box as in steps 1 and 2 of the Dome Chest, page 41, and let dry.

2 Apply double-sided adhesive to the back of all papers.

3 Cut black cardstock into pieces that measure: 3½" x 4½" and 2" x 3½".

4 Cut Tan Gator paper to measure 2½" x 4½".

5 Center and apply the Tan Gator paper to the 3½" x 4½" black cardstock piece.

6 Continue the layered stack by centering and applying the 2" x 3½" black cardstock piece to the top of the Tan Gator piece, as shown.

7 Adhere the layered stack to the top of the notepad box.

8 Punch four large gold teardrops, four small copper teardrops, and five ½" gold ribbon circles and adhere to the layered stack in the design shown in Figure 1.

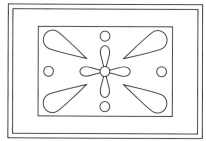

Figure 1

Three-Drawer Chest

MATERIALS

Papier-mâché three-drawer chest
   by MB Glick
DecoArt™ Americana® Acrylic Paint
   • 2 oz. bottle Raw Sienna
8 oz. jar DecoArt™ Faux Glazing
   Medium™ Clear Art Glaze
Emagination Crafts, Inc.™
   Bravissimo! Paper (8½" x 11")
   • 1 sheet Tan Gator
DMD Paper Reflections®
   • 1 sheet Black Cardstock
     (8½" x 11")
   • 1 sheet Gold Wave Metallic
     (8½" x 5")
   • 1 sheet Copper Metallic (4" x 4")
Emagination Crafts, Inc.™
   Craft Punches
   • Teardrop (large and small)
3 sheets permanent double-sided
   adhesive (8½" x 11")
Sea sponge
Tacky glue
Scissors or rotary cutter

INSTRUCTIONS

1 Sponge paint chest as in steps 1 and 2 of the Dome Chest, page 41, and let dry.

2 Apply double-sided adhesive to the back of all papers.

3 Cut the black cardstock to measure:
  • 2¾" square
  • 2¼" x 3¾"
  • 2¼" x 3¾"

4 Cut the Tan Gator paper to measure:
  • 2⅜" square
  • 1⅞" x 2½"
  • 1⅞" x 2½"

5 Center and apply 2⅜" Tan Gator square on top of 2¾" black cardstock square.

6 Adhere this square layered stack to the top of the chest.

7 Center and apply a 1½" x 2½" Tan Gator piece to the top of one 2½" x 3½" black cardstock piece. Repeat for the other two same-sized pieces.

9 Adhere these two layered pieces to each side of the chest.

J Punch six large black teardrops and six small copper teardrops.

K Center and layer each small copper teardrop on top of each large black teardrop.

L Apply the six layered teardrops to the front of the drawer fronts as shown in Figure 1 below.

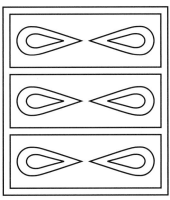

Figure 1

Letter Holder ◆

MATERIALS

Papier-mâché letter holder by MB Glick
DecoArt™ Americana® Acrylic Paint
  • 2 oz. bottle Raw Sienna
8 oz. jar DecoArt™ Faux Glazing
  Medium™ Clear Art Glaze
Emagination Crafts, Inc.™
  Bravissimo! Paper (8½" x 11")
  • 1 sheet Tan Gator
DMD Paper Reflections®
  • 1 sheet Black Cardstock
    (8½" x 11")
  • 1 sheet Gold Wave Metallic
    (8½" x 5")
  • 1 sheet Copper Metallic (4" x 4")
Emagination Crafts, Inc.™
  Craft Punches
  • Teardrop (large and small)
  • ¼" Circle (ribbon)
3 sheets permanent double-sided adhesive
  (8½" x 11")
Sea sponge
Tacky glue
Scissors or rotary cutter
Pencil

INSTRUCTIONS

1 Sponge paint box as in steps 1 and 2 of the Dome Chest, page 41, and let dry.

2 Apply double-sided adhesive to the back of all papers.

3 Trace the back arch of the letter holder onto scrap paper.

4 Trace the scrap paper pattern to the black cardstock and cut out the arch piece ⅛" smaller all the way around than the traced pencil line.

5 Trace the scrap paper pattern onto the Tan Gator paper and cut out the arch piece ¼" smaller all the way around than the traced pencil line.

6 Layer and adhere the Tan Gator arch piece on top of the black cardstock arch piece and apply this layered arch piece to the back arch of the letter holder.

7 Cut black cardstock into 1⅞" x 5⅞" and ⅞" x 3" pieces.

8 Cut Tan Gator paper into a 1⅛" x 4¼" piece.

9 Center and adhere the 1⅛" x 4¼" Tan Gator piece to the top of the 1⅞" x 5⅞" black cardstock piece, and then layer the ⅞" x 3" cardstock piece on top of the Tan

Gator. Attach this layered stack to front face of letter holder.

10 Punch two large gold teardrops, three small copper teardrops, and three ¼" copper ribbon circles.

11 Apply punches to layered front face of letter holder, as shown in Figure 1 below.

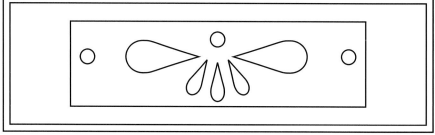

Figure 1

◆ Pencil Box, Pencils, and Pencil Cup

MATERIALS

For all projects combined:
Papier-mâché pencil box and square
    pencil cup by MB Glick
Pencils
DecoArt™ Americana® Acrylic Paint
• 2 oz. bottle Raw Sienna
8 oz. jar DecoArt™ Faux Glazing
    Medium™ Clear Art Glaze
Emagination Crafts, Inc.™
    Bravissimo! Paper (8½" x 11")
• 2 sheets Tan Gator
DMD Paper Reflections®
• 2 sheets Black Cardstock (8½" x 11")
• 1 sheet Gold Wave Metallic
    (8½" x 5")
• 1 sheet Copper Metallic (4" x 4")
Emagination Crafts, Inc.™
    Craft Punches
• Teardrop (large and small)
• ½" Circle (ribbon)
6 sheets permanent double-sided adhesive
    (8½" x 11")
Sea sponge
Tacky glue
Scissors or rotary cutter

INSTRUCTIONS

For Pencil Box and Pencils:

1 Sponge paint pencil box as in steps 1 and 2 of the Dome Chest, page 41, and let dry.

2 Apply double-sided adhesive to the back of all papers.

3 Cut two 1⅛" x 4" strips from black cardstock.

4 Cut two ⅞" x 4" strips from Tan Gator paper.

5 Center and apply each Tan Gator strip to the top of each black cardstock strip.

6 Wrap and adhere each layered strip to the pencil box, as shown.

7 With the remainder of the Tan Gator sheet, cut 1¼" x 6⅞" strips.

You should be able to get eight strips. Note that the length of the paper strip will vary with the length of your pencil; our pencils were 6⅞" long from the unsharpened ends to just overlapping the metal bands at the eraser ends.

8 Wrap and adhere each strip around a pencil.

For Pencil Cup:

1 Sponge paint pencil box as done for the pencil box.

2 Apply double-sided adhesive to the back of all papers.

3 Cut black cardstock into two 1½" x 3" pieces and one 2" x 3" piece.

4 Cut Tan Gator paper into two 1½ " x 2½" pieces.

5 Center and layer each of the Tan Gator pieces to the tops of each of the 1½" x 3" black cardstock pieces.

6 Center and adhere each of these layers to the pencil cup sides, as shown in the photo that follows.

7 Punch four large gold tear-drops, four ½" gold ribbon circles, four small copper teardrops, and one ½" copper ribbon circles.

8 Arrange the punches on top of the 2" x 3" black cardstock piece as shown in Figure 1 and adhere to the front of the pencil cup.

Figure 1

Large File Chest ◆

MATERIALS

10½" x 9½" x 8" papier-mâché chest by MB Glick
DecoArt™ Americana® Acrylic Paint
  • 2 oz. bottle Raw Sienna
8 oz. jar DecoArt™ Faux Glazing Medium
Emagination Crafts, Inc.™ Bravissimo! Paper (8½" x 11")
  • 5 sheets Tan Gator
DMD Paper Reflections®
  • 5 sheets Black Cardstock (8½" x 11")
  • 1 sheet Gold Wave Metallic (8½" x 5")
  • 1 sheet Copper Metallic (4" x 4")
Emagination Crafts, Inc.™ Craft Punches
  • Circle (super jumbo, large, and small)
  • Square (super jumbo)
  • Teardrop (large and small)
  • ½" Circle (ribbon)
Fiskars® Shapecutter
  • Ovals
  • Circles
Emagination Crafts, Inc.™ Sticker Stock (½" self-adhesive single letter; I used "P" for the first initial of my last name.)
7 sheets permanent double-sided adhesive (8½" x 11")
Ruler
Cutting mat
Rotary cutter or craft knife
Pencil
Tacky glue

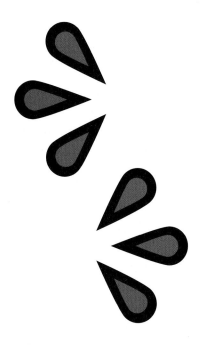

INSTRUCTIONS

1 Paint outside of chest with Raw Sienna and let dry.
2 Apply double-sided adhesive to all black cardstock and Tan Gator paper.

For the top of the file chest:
1 Cut black cardstock into one 9⅝" x 8" piece and one 7⅝" x 5" piece.
2 Cut Tan Gator paper into one 8⅞" x 7¼" piece and one 6⅝" x 4" piece.
3 Center and apply the 6⅝" x 4" Tan Gator piece to the top of the 7⅝" x 5" black cardstock piece.
4 Center and apply the above layer to the 8⅞" x 7¼" Tan Gator piece.
5 Center and apply the three-piece layer to the final 9⅝" x 8"

black cardstock piece and then apply the entire stack to the top of the box.
6 Punch one super jumbo square from black cardstock, one large Gold Wave Metallic circle, one small Copper Metallic circle, and one black cardstock ¼" circle.
7 Center and glue the copper circle to the gold circle and the black circle to the center of the copper circle.
8 Center and glue the layered circle stack to the black square, as shown in Figure 1 on next page.
9 Referring to Figure 2 on next page, glue the entire circle-square stack to the box top as shown.
10 Punch six large black cardstock teardrops and six small Copper Metallic teardrops.

11 Center and glue each copper teardrop to each black teardrop.

12 Again referring to Figures 1 and 2 below, glue the teardrops as shown on each side of the layered circle-square.

<u>Fore the sides of the file chest:</u>

1 Cut two 7¼" x 5" pieces and two 7¼" x 2¼" pieces from black cardstock.

2 Cut two 6½" x 4⅜" pieces and two 6⅝" x 2" pieces from Tan Gator paper.

3 Center and apply each 6½" x 4⅜" Tan Gator piece to the tops of each 7¼" x 5" black piece.

4 Apply one of these stacks to each of the side portions below the lid crease.

5 Trace the arch on the side of the chest onto a plain piece of paper, cut this piece out to use as a template, and fold the arch template in half to mark the center.

6 Measure and mark the center of the two 7¼" x 2¼" black pieces.

7 Match the paper arch template center to the center mark of one 7¼" x 2¼" black cardstock piece, trace the arch, and cut it out. Do the same on the other 7¼" x 2¼" black cardstock piece.

8 Repeat step 7 for each of the 6⅝" x 2" Tan Gator pieces as well.

9 Center and apply each Tan Gator arch piece to each black cardstock arch piece.

10 Apply one arch stack to each side of the chest, above the lid crease, as shown in the photo.

<u>For the front of the file chest:</u>

1 From black cardstock, cut one 7¼" x 5" piece and one 9⅝" x 5" piece.

2 From Tan Gator paper, cut one 6½" x 4⅜" piece and one 8⅞" x 4¼" piece.

3 Center and apply the 6½" x 4⅜" Tan Gator piece to the 7¼" x 5" black piece and the 8⅞" x 4¼" Tan Gator piece to the 9⅝" x 5" black piece.

4 Center and apply the smaller Tan Gator-black stack to the front of the chest, above the lid crease.

5 Center and apply the larger Tan Gator-black stack to the chest front, below the lid crease.

6 Using the Shapecutter, cut a black cardstock oval approximately 4⅜" x 3½" and then a Gold Wave oval approximately ¼" smaller, all the way around, than the black cardstock oval.

7 Using the Shapecutter center cut a circle from the Gold Wave oval approximately 2⅛" in diameter.

8 Using the cutout Gold Wave circle piece, punch a super jumbo circle.

Super Jumbo Square   Small Copper Circle

Large Gold Circle   ¼" Black Circle

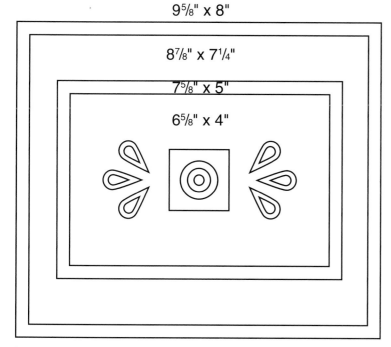

Figure 1

9⅝" x 8"

8⅞" x 7¼"

7⅝" x 5"

6⅝" x 4"

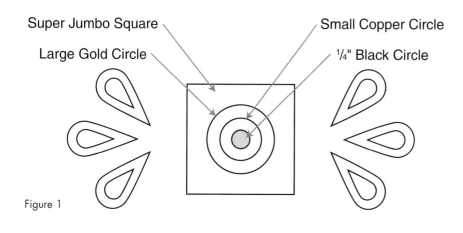

Figure 2

Continued on next page

9 Referring to Figure 3 at right, center and apply the Gold Wave oval to the black oval and the Gold Wave super jumbo circle to the cutout center of the Gold Wave oval so that some of the black cardstock shows through equally around the edges of the punched circle.

10 Center and apply the letter sticker to the center super jumbo Gold Wave punch circle.

11 Punch six large black cardstock teardrops and six small Copper Metallic teardrops.

12 Center and glue each copper teardrop to each black teardrop.

13 Again referring to Figure 3 for placement, glue the teardrop stacks to each side of the center oval-circle stack.

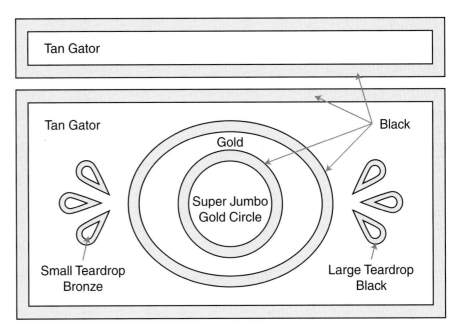

Figure 3

◆ Desk Lamp

MATERIALS

Purchased lamp with glass shade
Large olive jar, or any jar with a top that fits into the shade socket. (The one I used was 6" tall and narrow enough for an 8½" x 11" paper sheet to fit around.)
1 sheet Bravissimo! Copper Handmade Indian Paper by Emagination Crafts, Inc.™ (8½" x 11")
18 gold metallic eyelets by Emagination Crafts, Inc.™
⅛" hole punch
Eyelet setter
4 to 8 assorted gold, copper, and black beads from the Beadery
36" black Natural Hemp Cording Natural Knots™ by Toner Plastics
Pencil

INSTRUCTIONS

1 Remove the glass shade from the lamp and replace it with the olive jar, as shown below.

2 Hold Copper Handmade Indian Paper horizontally and tear edges to give a deckled look.
3 Place paper snuggly around jar, matching deckled edges.

4 With a pencil, lightly mark a line on both ends where the papers come together. Use this line to help determine eyelet placement.
5 Punch ⅛" holes down the line, approximately 1" apart and erase the guide line.
6 Add eyelets to the holes.

7 Thread cord into top circle and pull through until cord ends meet

evenly. The cord will be equal front and back.
8 Lace cord down both sides of the shade.
9 Tie an overhand knot with both cords at the bottom of the shade.
10 Add beads.
11 Tie an overhand knot below the beads, as shown below, and trim the ends leaving a 2" fringe.

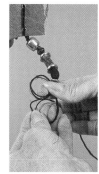

CHAPTER 6

PROJECTS FOR YOUR KITCHEN

As you head for that first cup of morning coffee, feel as though you've traveled to the farm as you're greeted by a rooster—minus the sound effects!

Roosters are so popular in home décor but can be expensive. Not so with the projects in this chapter, which features not only the rooster, but also a hen and an egg! And to help with the age-old dilemma: It doesn't matter which project you attempt first, the chickens or the egg.

The kitchen stools add a little whimsy, while the kitchen cupboard and quilt-look floor cloth projects continue the country theme.

All these projects can be made to work in your décor by a change in color. Stick with the red, white, and black, or try a more sophisticated look with blues and beiges. The beauty of the projects in this book is that you have the choice to change color or punches to match your own style!

Black-and-White 3-D Rooster ◆

MATERIALS

Wooden base with ½" x 12" wooden
 dowel
Plastifoam® by Syndicate Sales
 • 3 discs (12" x 1")
 • 2 cones (4" x 9")
DecoArt™ Americana® Acrylic Paint
 • 2 oz. bottle Dark Pine Green
Artistic Wire™
 • 2 45"-long pieces 14-gauge tinned
  copper wire
 • 25 yards 16-gauge black wire
Emagination Crafts, Inc.™ Craft Punches
 • Teardrop (ribbon)
 • Hawthorne Leaf (jumbo)
 • White Oak Leaf (jumbo)
 • Grapevine Leaf (jumbo)
 • Impatien Leaf (jumbo and large)
 • Primitive Heart (large)
 • Holly Leaf (super jumbo)
 • Water Splat (super jumbo)

Decorative papers (8½" x 11")
 • 2 sheets solid yellow
 • 3 sheets assorted green prints
  (one light, one dark, and one in a
  medium hue)
 • 3 sheets assorted red-and-white
  prints (one solid and two mostly
  red with white)
 • 10 sheets assorted black-and-white
  prints (include prints with: mostly
  black, mostly white, and gray, i.e.
  black and white mixed with grayed
  tones)

Corrugated paper by DMD Paper
 Reflections® (8½" x 11")
 • 3 sheets Black
 • 1 sheet Red Low
2 Darice®13mm Easy-Glu Eyes
Tacky glue
Serrated knife
4 oz. jar gloss decoupage medium
Low-temperature glue gun and glue sticks
4 wooden toothpicks
Paintbrush

INSTRUCTIONS

1 Using the pattern on page 57
and serrated knife, cut the same
size notch out of all three
Plastifoam discs. As shown in
Figure 1, the cut-
out will be
slightly more
than a 45-
degree angle.
This is the
rooster's body.

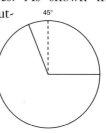

Figure 1

*Tip: Keep the cutout
pieces of Plastifoam to use
later for the beak and as
"sandpaper" to round off
corners on head.*

2 Using tacky glue, glue the three
body discs together in a stacked-
on-top-of-one-another fashion
and let dry.

3 For each of the cones, cut a piece out of the large end approximately halfway across the width and 5" down. See Figure 2 for guidance. These are the legs. Use a scrap piece of foam as sand paper to round off the top of the thighs.

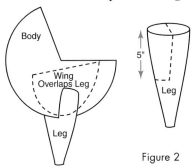

Figure 2

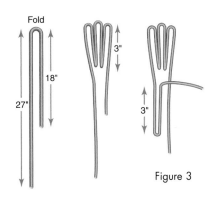

Figure 3

2 Twist the remaining wire together to form the lower leg/bird ankle.
3 Cut two 5-yard pieces from the 16-gauge black wire.
4 Fold over 1" of the end of the black wire.
5 Starting with the back toe, wrap the black wire around the far end of the 14-gauge wire toe and wrap towards the lower leg/bird ankle.

Continued on next page

For the legs:

1 Begin covering the legs at the small end. Adhere punches with tacky glue to the Plastifoam legs by layering in the following pattern:

- Two layers of mostly black paper White Oak Leaves, requiring approximately 12 punches.
- One layer of gray paper Hawthorne Leaves, requiring approximately 10 punches.
- Three layers of black-and-white paper Grapevine Leaves, requiring approximately 30 punches.
- Three layers of gray paper White Oak Leaves, requiring approximately 45 punches.

2 Cover the remaining thigh with mostly black paper White Oak Leaves, which will require approximately 100 punches.

For the body:

1 Cover the chest area starting at the back of the rooster with mostly black paper Impatien Leaves, which will require approximately 300 punches.

2 Cover the sides and the back with mostly white paper Grapevine Leaves, which will require approximately 500 punches. Leave the head for later.

For the feet:

1 Using Figure 3 as your guide, take one piece of 14-gauge wire and form four 3" toes.

Note: When you are choosing your decorative papers, think about how they are going to be used.

The yellow paper will be the beak, so it needs to be solid or a print that reads like solid.

The green will be the grass at the base of the rooster; you need a light, medium, and dark green solid or print that's not busy. I used a mottled tone-on-tone paper for my greens.

The reds will be for the waddle and comb. I used a combination of solid red and mostly red with a little white print to add some interest.

The blacks and whites are the most important papers and are used to shade the rooster. The white papers are used for the head and chest. These papers are the lightest of the feathers and need to be prints that are mostly white with some black. The chest and body are darker and need to be a strong black-and-white print. The chest papers are prints that are more black and the body printers are lighter. The wing feathers are a solid white paper topped with mostly black print.

Examine the leg in the photo and see how they are shaded in three colors. The top leg is dark, a mostly black print. The next section is a black print that includes gray and white. You will want a visual difference in the shades of these papers. The next section of the leg is the lightest shade and I used a repeat paper I had used on the body. Then you repeat the gray print and black.

The tail feathers are also shaded. You can see the darker prints are used at the top and closest to the body. As you move toward the back, you'll note I used lighter prints.

You can use scraps that you already have or use all new papers for this project. You could even use more prints or all the same print for one section, if you like. The color choices are yours!

Keep the wrap tight and cover all but the very end of the toe.

6 Pull wire to the front of each toe, and then wrap back toward the leg.

7 Wrap wire five or six times around where all of the toes meet. Then wrap up the leg.

8 Attach the foot to the legs by pushing the remaining 14-gauge wire up through the bottom of the Plastifoam leg and glue the leg to hold it in place.

9 Repeat the entire process for the other foot.

J Insert two wooden toothpicks into center of inner thigh. Place one toothpick above the other and insert them about halfway into the foam.

K Apply tacky glue to the exposed area and apply to the body, holding for a few minutes until the glue sets. Repeat for the second leg.

For the wings:

1 From the black 16-gauge wire, cut nine 5"-long pieces.

2 Using the super jumbo Holly Leaves, cover five wires with about 100 mostly black with white dot paper punches and four wires with about 100 more mostly black plaid print paper punches. Note: Each wire piece is covered by starting at one end and covering both sides of the wire with punches. Punches will be placed both right-side up and wrong-side up. This way the leaves fit together when placed on wires.

3 Using the Wing Pattern on page 56, cut out main wing from corrugated paper.

4 With the glue gun, glue the punch-covered wires to the end of the wing so that they appear to be individual feathers extending off the edge of the main wing.

5 Cover the remaining portion of the main wing with a layer of mostly black Impatien Leaves (approximately 80 punches) on top of mostly white Impatien Leaves (approximately 80 more punches), as shown in Figure 4.

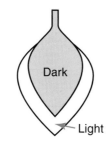

Figure 4

Dark

Light

6 Glue the wing to one side of the rooster with the glue gun.

7 Repeat the entire process for the other wing.

For the tail feathers:

1 Cut 16-gauge black wire as follows: seven 14" pieces, seven 9" pieces, and five 8" pieces.

2 Starting at the end and working your way down, cover all the 14" wires with Grapevine Leaves using about 350 black-and-white zebra print punches, 350 middle gray print punches, and another 350 base black with small white print punches. Be sure to cover both sides of the wires with reverse leaves as discussed in step 2 of the wing section and leave 2" to 3" at one end for insertion into the Plastifoam.

3 In the same fashion as the 14" wires, cover the 9" wires with approximately 210 gray print Grapevine Leaf punches and the 8" wires with 100 mostly white print Grapevine Leaf punches.

4 Coat all tail feathers with gloss medium before adding to body.

5 Push the 8" wires into the body just below the back end, spacing them slightly apart. Glue to Plastifoam.

6 Push the 9" wires into the body just where the top ends, spacing them slightly apart. Glue to Plastifoam.

7 The 14" wires should be pushed into the back approximately 2" and 3"toward the front, spacing them slightly apart. Glue to Plastifoam.

8 Bend the tail feathers into a curve over the back.

For the head:

1 Using the Rooster Head

Template on page 57, cut the head out of black corrugated paper and glue it into a cone shape.

2 Using approximately 300 mostly white print Water Splat punches, start at the bottom and cover the head and the neck evenly over the top of the wings.

3 With the glue gun, glue head to the top of the body.

4 Using the Beak Pattern on page 56, cut the beak from the earlier leftover Plastifoam scraps.

5 Starting from the point, cover the beak piece with approximately 45 solid yellow Primitive Heart punches.

6 Punch two black teardrop punch nostrils and glue to the sides of the beak.

7 Glue the beak approximately 1" down from the top of the head.

8 Using the patterns on page 56, cut the comb and the waddle out of red corrugated paper. Cut two of each part.

9 Glue the two pieces together.

10 Cover the comb and waddle pieces with approximately 350 red-and-white print punched Oak Leaves.

11 With the glue gun, glue the comb to the top of the head, the waddle below the beak, and the eyes to the head, as shown here.

Finishing the project:

1 Paint the base and the dowel Dark Pine Green and let dry.

2 Using the glue gun, mount the roster on the dowel.

3 Make grass using approximately 120 super jumbo Holly Leaf punches from the green papers and glue close around base, as shown in the photo at right.

4 Coat the rooster with five to eight coats of gloss medium. Let dry thoroughly between coats.

Basic Rooster Parts Diagram

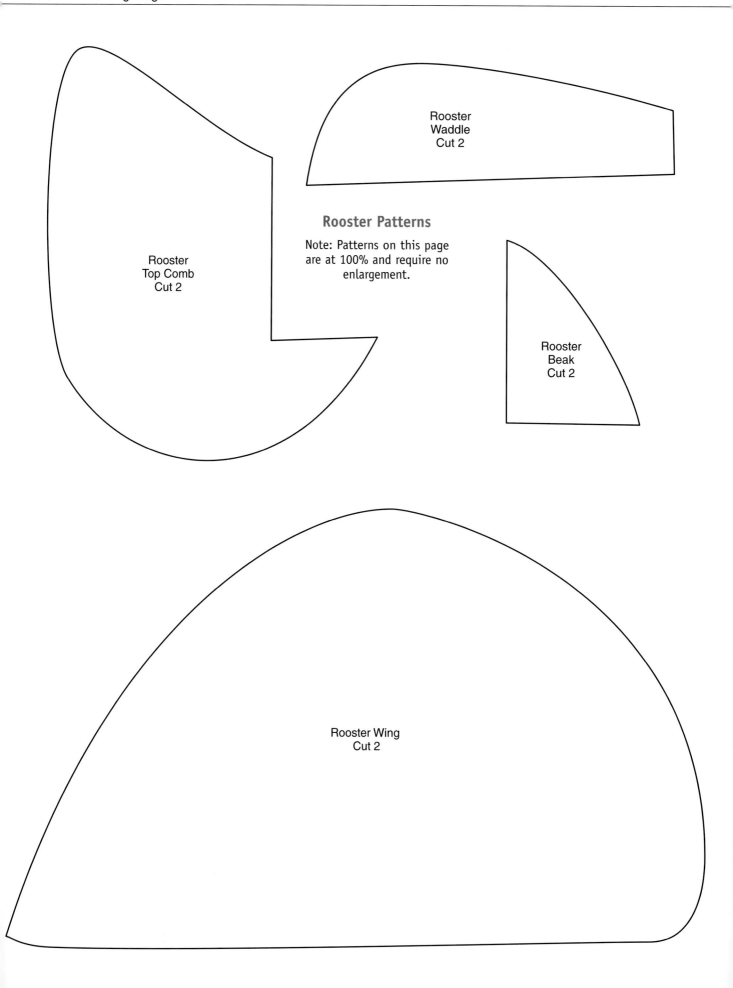

Rooster
Waddle
Cut 2

Rooster Patterns

Note: Patterns on this page are at 100% and require no enlargement.

Rooster
Top Comb
Cut 2

Rooster
Beak
Cut 2

Rooster Wing
Cut 2

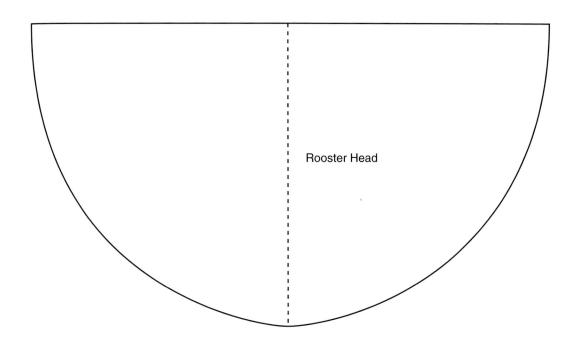

Rooster Head

Rooster Patterns

Enlarge 200%

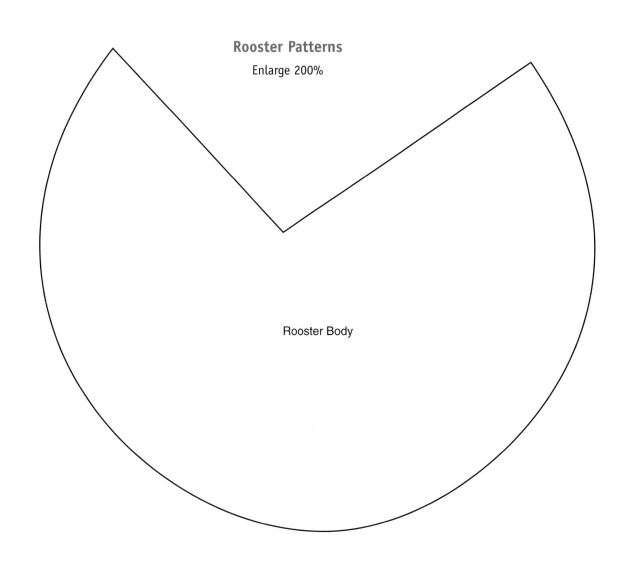

Rooster Body

Black-and-White Hen

MATERIALS

Wooden base with ½" x 8" wooden dowel
Plastifoam® by Syndicate Sales
- 3 discs (12" x 1")
- 1 4" ball

Artistic Wire™
- 2 45"-long pieces 14-gauge tinned copper wire
- 7 yards 16-gauge black wire

DecoArt™ Americana® Acrylic Paint
- 2 oz. bottle Dark Pine Green

Emagination Crafts, Inc.™ Craft Punches
- Teardrop (ribbon)
- Hawthorne Leaf (jumbo)
- White Oak Leaf (jumbo)
- Grapevine Leaf (jumbo)
- Impatien Leaf (jumbo and large)
- Primitive Heart (large)
- Holly Leaf (super jumbo)
- Water Splat (super jumbo)

Decorative papers (8½" x 11")
- 1 sheet solid yellow
- 3 sheets assorted red-and-white prints (one solid and two mostly red with white)
- 10 sheets assorted black-and-white prints (include prints with: mostly black, mostly white, and gray, i.e. black and white mixed with grayed tones)

Corrugated paper by DMD Paper Reflections® (8½" x 11")
- 4 sheets Black
- 1 sheet Red

2 Darice®15mm Easy-Glu Eyes
Tacky glue
Serrated knife
4 oz. jar gloss decoupage medium
Low-temperature glue gun and glue sticks
Paintbrush

INSTRUCTIONS

For the body:

1 Using the serrated knife and the pattern on page 61, cut body pattern out of three large Plastifoam discs.

2 Using tacky glue, glue pieces together as shown in Figure 1, and let dry.

Tip: Keep the cutout pieces of Plastifoam to use later for the beak and as sandpaper to round off corners on head.

Figure 1

3 Cut 4" ball into three equal pieces. Discard the center piece.

4 Glue the two sides of the ball on either side of the hen body as indicated in Figure 1.

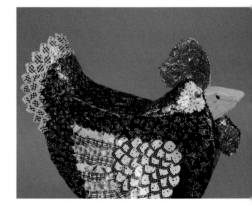

5 Cover the body, starting at the tail end, with approximately 800 mostly black print Grapevine Leaf punches. Overlap the punches as you go.

For the wings:
1 Cut the wings out of black corrugated paper using the Rooster Wing Pattern on page 61.
2 Cover each wing with alternating rows of black-and-white plaid paper super jumbo Holly Leaf punches and the gray prints. You will need approximately 100 punches in each paper for each wing; for example, 200 total black-and-white plaid super jumbo Holly Leaf punches and 200 total gray print super jumbo Holly Leaf punches.
3 Before adhering the punches to the corrugated wings, back the Holly Leaf punches with mirror-image punches of the same print. To punch mirror image punches, first punch the right side of the paper up, and then turn the paper over and punch the wrong side up.
4 Continue alternating Holly Leaf rows until half of each wing is covered in punches, which will take about 11 rows to accomplish.
5 Cover the other halves of the wings with double layers of Impatien Leaves. For the bottom layer, use 40 jumbo Impatien Leaf punches from mostly black print paper. The top layer is 40 large Impatien Leaf punches from mostly white print paper.
6 Use the glue gun to glue each wing over the balls on the sides of the body.

For the tail:
1 Using the tailpiece pattern on page 60, cut two tailpieces out of black corrugated paper.
2 Glue the curved piece over the top end of the hen, and glue the inset piece behind it and to the back of the hen.
3 Cover the backside of the tail with approximately 80 punches to match those used on the hen's body.
4 On the front side of the tail, make three rows of the two Impatien Leaves stacked on top of each other. The larger bottom leaves will be jumbo Impatien Leaf punches from mostly white print (approximately 60 punches) and the smaller leaves on top will be large Impatien Leaf punches from mostly black print (another 60 punches).
5 Adhere these rows from the end of the tail moving each row toward the body.
6 Continuing toward the body, follow these three rows with three or four rows of doubled Impatien Leaf punches with 60 jumbo punches of mostly black paper and 60 large punches from gray print.

For the head:
1 Using the beak pattern on page 60, cut the beak from the earlier leftover Plastifoam.
2 Cover the Plastifoam with about 60 yellow Primitive Heart punches, starting at the point and working toward the larger end.
3 Punch two black teardrop nostrils and glue to the sides of the beak.
Glue the beak approximately 1" down from the top of the head.
4 Using the patterns on page 60, cut the comb and the waddle out of red corrugated paper. Cut two of each part.
5 Glue the two pieces together for the comb.
6 Cover the comb and waddle with about 100 red-and-white print punched Oak Leaves.
7 With the glue gun, glue the comb to the top of the head, and the waddle below the beak.
8 Cover the eye area with Hawthorne Leaf punches out of mostly white print by first placing one leaf in the center and overlapping leaf punches in a circle around the first leaf. You will need approximately 10 leaves per eye.

9 Glue the eyes on top of the Hawthorne Leaf punch area.

For the feet:
1 Referring to Figure 3 in the Black-and-White 3-D Rooster project as your guide (page 53), take one piece of 14-gauge wire and form four 3" toes.
2 Twist the remaining wire together to form the lower leg/bird ankle.
3 Cut two 5-yard pieces from the 16-gauge black wire.
4 Fold over 1" of the end of the black wire.
5 Starting with the back toe, wrap the black wire around the far end of the 14-gauge wire toe and wrap towards the lower leg/bird ankle. Keep the wrap tight and cover all but the very end of the toe.
6 Pull wire to the front of each toe, and then wrap back toward the leg.
7 Wrap wire five or six times around where all of the toes meet. Then wrap up the leg.
8 Attach the foot to the body by pushing the remaining 14-gauge wire up through the bottom of the Plastifoam and glue the foot to hold it in place.
9 Repeat the entire process for the other foot.

Finishing the project:
1 Paint the wood pieces Dark Pine Green and let dry.
2 Stick the dowel into the wood and the other end into the hen. Glue into place with the glue gun. Cover everything with three to five coats of gloss medium. Let dry between coats.

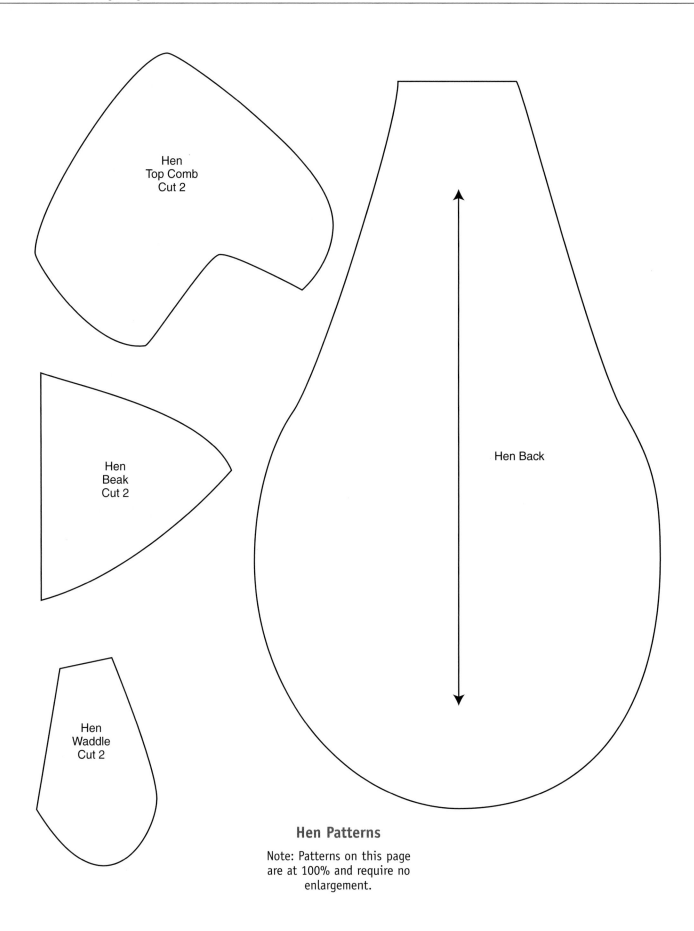

Hen
Top Comb
Cut 2

Hen Back

Hen
Beak
Cut 2

Hen
Waddle
Cut 2

Hen Patterns

Note: Patterns on this page
are at 100% and require no
enlargement.

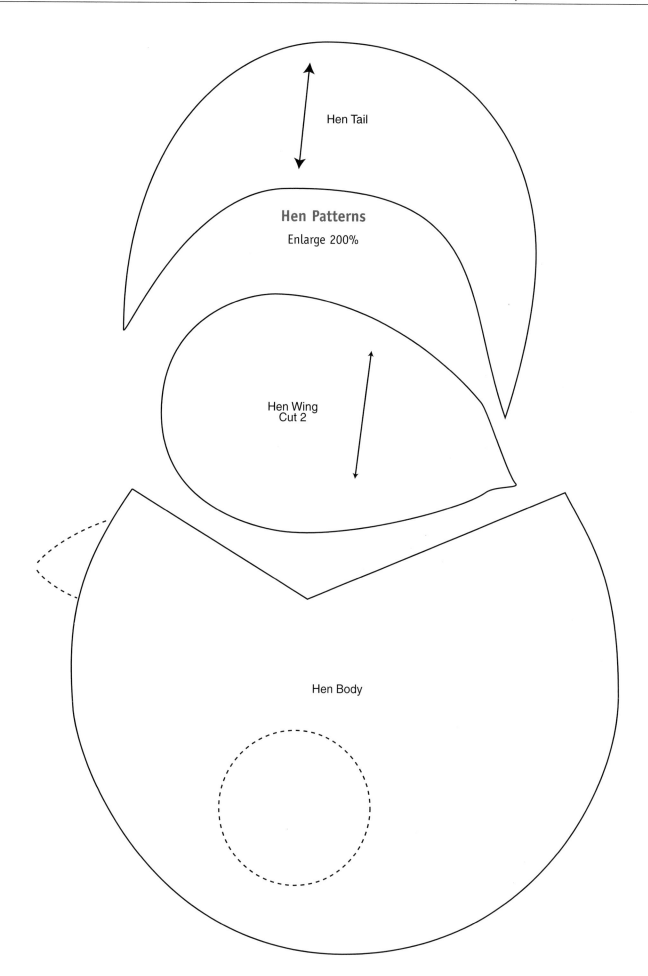

Hen Tail

Hen Patterns

Enlarge 200%

Hen Wing
Cut 2

Hen Body

Kitchen Floor Cloth ◆

MATERIALS

32½" x 24½" Kreative Kanvas II®
DecoArt™ Americana® Acrylic Paint
- 2 oz. bottle White
- 2 oz. bottle Black

8 oz. can DecoArt™ Americana®
    Polyurethane Varnish
Emagination Crafts, Inc.™ Craft Punches
- Square (super giant and jumbo)

Decorative papers (8½" x 11")
- 8 sheets assorted black-and-white prints
- 6 to 8 sheets assorted red prints
- 3 sheets assorted yellow prints

DMD Paper Reflections®
- 1 sheet Red Cardstock (8½" x 11")

Permanent adhesive
1"-wide painters' tape
Paintbrush
Rotary cutter
Cutting mat
Ruler

INSTRUCTIONS

1 Paint canvas white and let dry.

2 Using painters' tape, mark off a 1" border around canvas edge.

3 Paint border black, let dry, and remove tape.

4 Using painters' tape, mark off a 2¼" white border inside the black border. Paint, as shown below, let dry, and remove tape, as shown.

5 Inside the white border, mark off a ½"-wide black border.

6 Using the rotary cutter, cut 32 4" squares from black-and-white print paper.

7 Apply squares to the center portion of the rug, as shown in the photo below, completing the design with partial squares applied along the edges of the rug.

8 Punch 22 solid red jumbo squares from cardstock and apply these red squares to where the corners of the black-and-white squares meet, as shown below.

9 Measure and cut four 2¼" red cardstock squares and apply to corners.

10 Punch four red print super giant squares and adhere to the center tops of the 2¼" red corner squares.

11 Punch 38 assorted red and yellow print papers with the super giant square punch.

12 Apply the assorted red and yellow squares on the white border at diamond angles. See photo below for design details.

13 Apply several coats of varnish.

◆ Decoupage Egg

MATERIALS

8" papier-mâché egg by DCC
DecoArt™ Americana® Polyurethane
   Gloss Varnish
DecoArt™ Americana® Acrylic Paint
   • 2 oz. bottle Black
Handmade Paper by DMD Paper
   Reflections® (8½" x 11")
   • 5 sheets Black and Gold Lattice
   • 5 sheets Nepal Lokta Red
Emagination Crafts, Inc.™ Craft Punches
   • Heart (super jumbo)
   • Water Splat (super jumbo)
Permanent adhesive
Paintbrush

> *Tip: Repeat designs are a great way to cover objects in any size or shape.*
>
> *I like to use two different punches and two different papers in combination.*
>
> *First, make the pair combinations, as shown in Figure 1 below. Then, begin at one end of your object, overlapping the punches until the piece is completely covered.*

INSTRUCTIONS

1 Paint the egg black. Let dry.
2 Punch approximately 120 Nepal Lokta Red water splats and 120 Black and Gold Lattice hearts.

3 Adhere each water splat punch on top of each heart punch, as shown in Figure 1.

Figure 1

4 Starting at the small end of the egg, apply the water splat-hearts with heart tip pointing up so that they meet at the point of the egg.
5 Start layering around the egg toward the large end.

6 When egg is completely covered, apply several coats of varnish.

Bar Stools ◆

MATERIALS

Unfinished wood bar stool

DecoArt™ Americana® Acrylic Paint
- 2 oz. bottle White
- 2 oz. bottle Calico Red

8 oz. can DecoArt™ Americana® Satin Polyurethane Varnish

Emagination Crafts, Inc.™ The Edge™ Pinking Scissors

Emagination Crafts, Inc.™ Craft Punches
- Circle (¼" ribbon, ⅛" ribbon, and small)
- Rectangle (ribbon)
- Teardrop (small and large)
- Square (large)
- Water Splat (large and super jumbo)

Large Swirl Craft Punch by Punch Bunch™

Cardstock by DMD Paper Reflections® (8½" x 11")
- 1 sheet Black
- 1 sheet Burgundy
- 4 sheets Red
- 1 sheet Marigold
- 1 sheet White

Tacky glue

Zig Calligraphy Extra Pen (waterproof pigment ink)

Paintbrush

INSTRUCTIONS

1 Paint the entire stool with two coats of white paint and let dry.

2 Paint the seat only in two coats of Calico Red. Let dry.

3 Use the small end of the calligraphy pen to mark the stool into four quarters. Make a line that looks like a stitching line, using the flat side of the pen to draw small stitches as shown below. Be sure to mark down the seat's sides.

4 Punch 50 large red cardstock swirls (25 on each side) and 100 marigold cardstock circles (50 on each side).

5 Use the ¼" marigold circles to pattern two sections of the seat.

6 Use the red textured paper swirls to pattern the remaining two quarters of the seat, as shown.

7 The five button designs consist of a super jumbo burgundy water splat on the bottom, layered next with a large black water splat, and then with a marigold small circle with two ⅛" circles punched side by side. The last layer is a white rectangle applied between the two holes to represent a stitch. Note: It is easier to punch the two ⅛" circles in the marigold paper first and then turn the small hole punch upside-down, centered on the two holes, and punch.

8 Adhere the button designs on the stool seat, placing one in the center and the other four on the stitch lines.

9 For the tassels, one of which will be placed on each leg, first punch the small teardrop in red paper. Then, with the punch centered over the hole, punch a large teardrop. This makes the top tassel loop.

10 Under this, place a small red circle.

11 Then cut at least four strips each of burgundy and red strips using the pinking scissors as shown below. Cut these strips approximately ⅛" x 2¼".

12 Glue the burgundy and red strips on each leg ½" below the small circle.

13 Punch a burgundy square and adhere it over the strip and slightly overlapping the small circle, as shown at right.

14 Add a burgundy ⅛"-wide strip from loop to the top of the stool leg, as shown in the photo that follows.

15 Use many light coats of varnish so that the paper punches are submerged in the finish and the top of the seat feels smooth.

Mosaic Watermelon Tray ◆

MATERIALS

12" x 16" rectangle tray
  by Walnut Hollow
DecoArt™ Americana® Acrylic Paint
  • 2 oz. bottle Black
8 oz. can DecoArt™ Americana®
  Polyurethane Varnish
Cardstock by DMD Paper Reflections®
  (8½" x 11")
  • 2 sheets Red
  • 1 sheet Light Olive
  • 2 sheets Christmas Green
  • 1 sheet Tan
6 sheets permanent adhesive
Paintbrush

INSTRUCTIONS

1 Paint the tray black and let dry.
2 Back all the cardstock sheets with adhesive.
3 Using the Watermelon Tray Pattern on the next page, trace the inside of the watermelon on the Red cardstock, the inner rind on Light Olive, and the outside rind on Christmas Green.
4 Cut the shapes into random pieces that look like broken tile and adhere to the tray.

5 Apply Tan cardstock pieces in the same broken tile fashion to form the background.
6 The lip of the tray has four rows of green stripes, alternating between the Christmas Green and the Light Olive. Refer to the main project photo above for design details.
7 Apply several coats of varnish to tray.

Watermelon Tray Pattern

Kitchen Cabinet ◆

MATERIALS

13½" wide x 31½" high x 10½" deep unfinished shaker cabinet by Walnut Hollow

Deco Art™ Americana® Acrylic Paint
- 2 oz. bottle Snow White
- 2 oz. bottle Calico Red
- 8 oz. can Deco Art™ Americana® Polyurethane Varnish

Emagination Crafts, Inc.™
Craft Punches
- Circle (½" ribbon, ½" ribbon, and small)
- Quasar (ribbon)
- Rectangle (ribbon)
- Teardrop (small and large)
- Square (large)

Large Swirl Punch by Punch Bunch™

Emagination Crafts, Inc.™ The Edge™ Scallop Scissors

Emagination Crafts, Inc.™ Bravissimo! Paper (8½" x 11")
- 3 sheets King

Cardstock by DMD Paper Reflections® (8½" x 11")
- 2 sheets Red
- 2 sheets Burgundy
- 2 sheets Marigold
- 2 sheets Black
- 4 sheets Grey Stone

Photocopies of pictures of cookies, candies, crackers, and real foliage (enough to fit in jars)

14 sheets double-sided permanent adhesive

Photocopier

Paintbrush

INSTRUCTIONS

1 Paint the cabinet completely with white paint and let dry.

2 Paint the top of the cabinet and a triangle on each side with red paint. See photo below for guidance with this step.

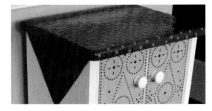

3 Punch 90 large swirls from red cardstock (45 per side).

4 Punch 160 ¼" circles from Marigold cardstock (80 per side).

5 Back all punches with adhesive.

6 Apply punches to the red portions of the cabinet in quartered-off triangular sections with the Marigold pieces placed in the top front and top back triangles and the red pieces on the top right and left triangles and the triangles on each side of the cabinet.

7 Following steps 9 through 14 of the Bar Stool project instructions (page 65), make tassels for each side of cabinet and place at point of triangle.

8 Cut eight jar patterns, page 70, from Grey Stone cardstock.

9 Cut seven jar lids only, page 70, from King paper.

10 Back all pieces with double-sided adhesive and apply four jars to the front cabinet doors and one to each side of the cabinet. One of the side jars will not have a lid; it will be filled with leaves.

11 Photocopy the items for the jars. Back with adhesive. Cut out the items and apply to jars.

12 To create the punched tin look on the front of the cabinet, run the wrong side of a sheet of King paper through a copier.

13 Copy the copy to be a mirror image. Trim off excess paper.

14 Punch all holes as shown in the Punched Tin Template, page 71.

15 Cut out hole for doorknob.

16 Apply adhesive to the right side of the black cardstock and attach the right side of the black cardstock to the wrong side of the punched tin paper.

17 Apply the double-sided adhesive to the back of the black cardstock and adhere to the cabinet doors as shown below.

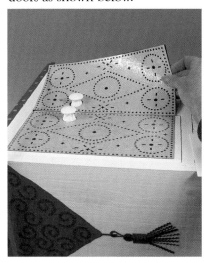

18 Apply many light coats of varnish.

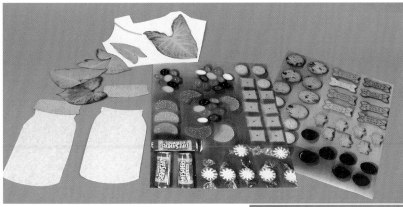

As outlined in step 11, photocopy the items for the jars, back with adhesive, and cut them out as shown at left. Then, arrange in the jars, similar to arrangements shown below.

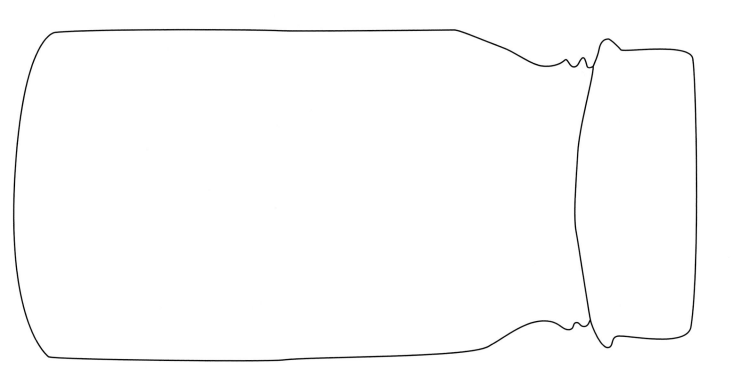

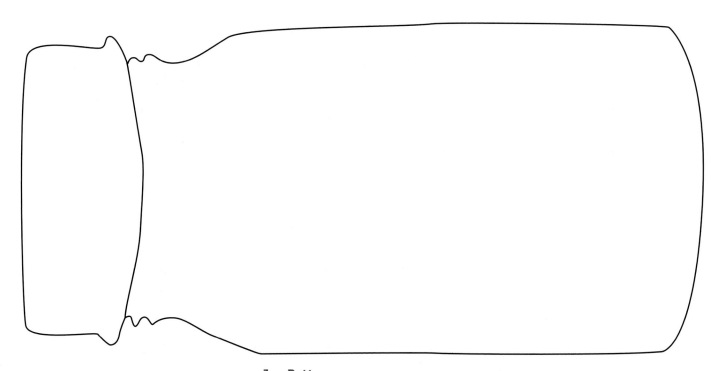

Jar Patterns

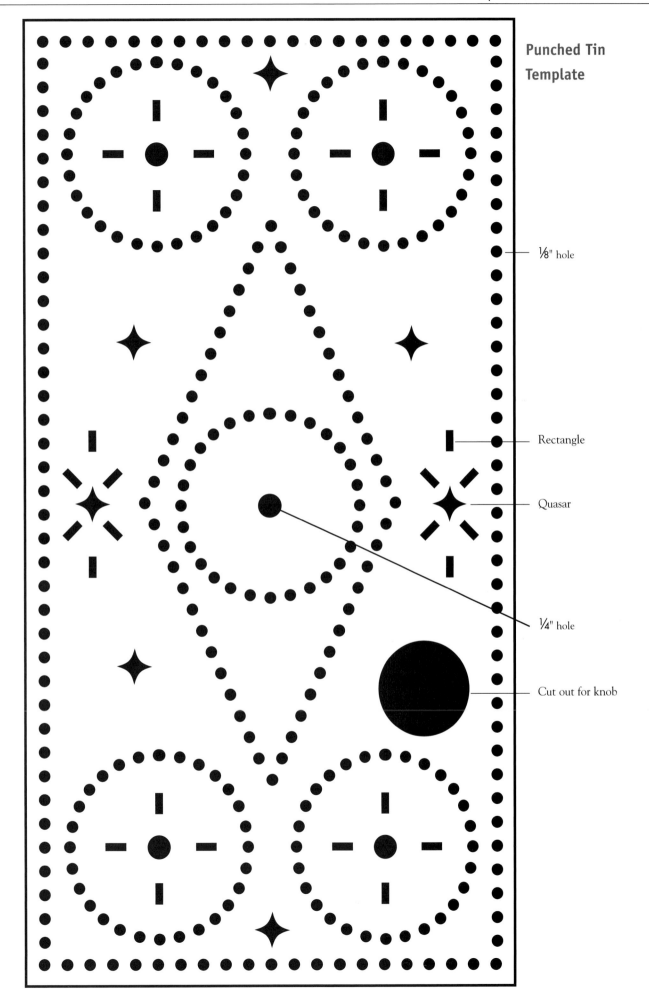

⅛" hole

Rectangle

Quasar

¼" hole

Cut out for knob

CHAPTER 7

PROJECTS FOR YOUR SITTING ROOM

A lady's sitting room with a touch of romance; it's lace and flowers and very Victorian.

Chintz dishes and teapots are all the rage in decorator magazines, but now you can make your own. Roam the fabric store and find a few fabrics that reflect your color scheme. Off to the local copy center and you can make your own custom decorative paper by making color copies of your fabric choices.

Flea market finds can be dressed up to give a vintage look to any décor. An old mirror and a single ladies shoe can add charm.

The Victorian theme is a major look in scrapbooking papers today. Look for vintage stripes, realistic and watercolor florals, and wallpaper patterns. These types of papers help to create the elegant room divider—a great piece to hide not-so-elegant exercise equipment!

Patchwork Tray ◆

MATERIALS

20½" x 12½" octagon Home Plates™
  hardwood veneer tray
  by Walnut Hollow
DecoArt™ Americana® Satins Acrylic
  Enamel
  • 8 oz. jar Light Willow
8 oz. can DecoArt™ Americana® Satins
  Polyurethane Varnish
Emagination Crafts, Inc.™ Craft Punches
  • Teardrop (small and large)
  • Heart (large)
  • Quilt Hexagon (super jumbo)
  • Quilt Diamond – 60º
    (super jumbo)
Fiskars® Wide Seagull Paper Edgers
40" cream-colored ¼"-wide picot-edged
  satin ribbon
Emagination Crafts, Inc.™
  Bravissimo! Paper (8½" x 11")
  • 2 sheets Citrine Line
  • 2 sheets Mint Green Ice
Prints by Anna Griffin and
  Making Memories (8½" x 11")
  • 2 sheets floral print
  • 2 sheets Victorian print
    (to coordinate with floral print)
  • 2 sheets light paper with lacy
    design
Permanent adhesive
Paintbrush

INSTRUCTIONS

1 Paint the tray with Light Willow paint and let dry.
2 Punch 24 assorted print hexagons. Arrange on the center portion of the tray in six rows of four hexagons each.
3 Fill in between hexagons with 12 Citrine Line and 12 Mint Green Ice diamond punches. Trim the diamonds for the sides and the bottom to square up the design, as shown in the photo below.

4 Trim green white lace paper to make a 1½" border around the design. This will probably take two sheets of paper, one for each side of the tray.
5 Trim the outer edge of the border with the Seagull Edgers.

6 Before adhering lace paper to tray, place 36 green print hearts behind each of the small loops in the edge of the design, as shown in the photo below.

7 Adhere lacy paper to tray.
8 Adhere hexagon pattern to tray.
9 Add adhesive-backed picot ribbon over rough edges where the center pattern meets the edge of the border.
10 Add 36 large teardrops and 36 small teardrops, all from green print, to edges, as shown in the photo.

11 Apply several coats of varnish to tray.

◆ Patchwork Teapot

MATERIALS

Unfinished wooden teapot
  by Walnut Hollow
DecoArt™ Americana® Satins
  Acrylic Enamel
  • 8 oz. jar Powder Pink
  • 8 oz. jar Light Willow
8 oz. can DecoArt™ Americana® Satins
  Polyurethane Varnish
Emagination Crafts, Inc.™ Craft Punch
  • Quilt Hexagon (super jumbo)
Paper by Anna Griffin (8½" x 11")
  • 2 sheets large Floral
  • 2 sheets Green Stripe
  • scrap Victorian print
    (coordinating color)
4 sheets plus a scrap double-sided
  permanent adhesive
Fiskars® Corkscrew Paper Edgers
Paintbrush
Scissors

INSTRUCTIONS

1 Paint the body of the teapot and the ball on top of the lid with Powder Pink paint and let dry.

2 Paint the remainder of the teapot (handle, spout, bottom feet, and lid) with Light Willow paint, as shown below, and let dry.

3 Using the Corkscrew Paper Edgers, cut four wavy strips of the Green Stripe paper with the stripes lying horizontally. Adhere two strips to each side of the teapot, as shown in the next photo.

4 Back the Floral paper with adhesive.

5 With scissors, cut out floral patterns (flowers) and adhere two to the sides, as shown below, and one small motif to the lid.

6 Punch one quilt hexagon from Victorian paper and apply to center of lid, as shown below.

7 Cut medium flower out with scissors and apply offset on hexagon.

8 With glue gun, adhere ball on top of flowered hexagon.

9 Apply many light coats of varnish to the teapot and the lid.

Mosaic Box

MATERIALS

Papier-mâché small dome chest
    by MB Glick
Photocopy of a photograph (6" square to
    be cut into a 3" x 4" oval)
Fiskars® Oval Cutter
Fiskars® Craft Mat
Glossy photos in two basic colors
    (I used blues and pinks.)
DecoArt™ Americana® Satins
    Acrylic Enamel
    • 8 oz. jar Soft White
Scissors
Double-sided adhesive
6" square Keep A Memory™ Mounting
    Adhesive by ThermOWeb
Paintbrush

Tip: Look through your leftover photos for the photos you will need to cut up for this project. The subject doesn't matter, just the basic color. You will need enough photos to fill the area to your satisfaction.

INSTRUCTIONS

1 Paint the chest with Soft White and let dry.
2 Back the photocopy with mounting adhesive.
3 Place photocopy on craft mat and use the oval cutter to cut a 3" x 4" oval.
4 Remove the paper backing from the adhesive on the oval photocopy and apply the photocopy to the center of the chest top about 1¼" from the front edge.
5 Cut an oval from the pink-colored photo approximately ¾" larger than the photocopy.
6 Cut a 3" x 4" oval out of the pink-colored photo oval you've just made so you are left with a pink doughnut shape.
7 Cut the pink doughnut shape to make framing tiles around the

photocopy. Cut the pieces to look like broken tiles. Glue them around the photocopy, as shown, leaving approximately ⅛" spacing between the photocopy and the other tiles.

8 Cut tiles out of pink-colored photos, cut tiles that are approximately ⅜" wide and glue them along the lid edge and the edges of the bottom part of the chest to form a border.

9 Place tiles about 8" apart.
10 Fill in the rest of the chest with blue pieces, as shown, or add larger pieces if you desire.

Tip: Cut the background blue into 1" squares (tile size) and then cut them into broken tile shapes.

House Lamp

MATERIALS

12" papier-mâché house box by DCC

DecoArt™ Americana® Satins
  Acrylic Enamel
  • 8 oz. jar Dark Ecru
  • 8 oz. jar Sage Green
DecoArt™ Americana® Acrylic Paint
  • 2 oz. bottle Milk Chocolate
  • 2 oz. bottle Forest Green
Emagination Crafts, Inc.™ Craft Punches
  • Oak Leaf (small)
  • Water Splat (small)
  • Flower (small)
  • Teardrop (small)
  • Square (large)
  • Circle (large)
  • Impatien Leaf (large and jumbo)
  • Renaissance Viterbo (jumbo)
  • Renaissance Chartres (jumbo)
  • Vivaldi (border)
Emagination Crafts, Inc. The Edge™
  Victorian Scissors
Emagination Crafts, Inc.™
  Bravissimo! Papers (8½" x 11")
  • 2 sheets Patina Gold-Gold Mine
  • 3 sheets Gun Metal-Fate
2 sheets Heavy Cream Vellum by
  Canson Paper (8½" x 11")
Cardstock by DMD Paper Reflections®
  (8½" x 11")
  • 2 sheets Forest Green
  • 1 sheet Dark Brown
1 sheet Hydrangea Print Paper by NRN
  (8½" x 11")
Permanent adhesive
Sea sponge
Light base with bulb
Scissors
Craft knife

INSTRUCTIONS

1 Use the sea sponge to sponge a light coating of Dark Ecru paint on the house, including roof and chimney, and let dry.

2 Use a sea sponge to sponge a light coating of Sage Green paint. Let some of the Dark Ecru paint show through. Let dry.

3 Dab Forest Green paint for grass and Milk Chocolate paint for the front walk.

Continued on next page

For the roof:

1 Cut 24 ½" x 8½" strips of Gun Metal paper and glue each strip along the edges of the roof. Trim to fit.

2 Punch 170 jumbo Impatient Leaves out of Patina Gold paper. Punch 170 large Impatient Leaves out of Gun Metal paper.

3 Apply the large leaves on top of the jumbo leaves with the stem ends matching and glue.

4 Start applying the leaf layers at the bottom edge of the roof and work upward. On the second row, apply the leaves between the leaves of the first row, as shown in Figure 1. Do not cover the chimney with punches.

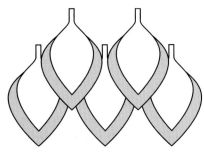

Figure 1

For the shutters:

1 Cut 24 2" x ¼" strips of Forest Green cardstock.

2 Align the Vivaldi border punch from the inside on each shutter. See the photo for shutter placement on the house.

For the windows:

1 Cut vellum to the size of each window plus 1".

2 Glue the vellum to the inside of

the house to cover each window panel.

3 For the decorative square windows, first punch the Renaissance Chartres punch into Dark Green cardstock and then center the large square punch to punch out the entire design. Punch a large square vellum piece and adhere to the back of the decorative square. Glue the design and glue to the house, as shown in photo at top of this column.

4 For the decorative round window, first punch the Renaissance Viterbo punch into the Dark Green cardstock and then center the large circle punch to punch out the entire design. Punch a  large circle vellum piece and adhere to the back of the decorative circle. Glue the design and glue it to the house in a diamond angle.

For the door:

1 Cut Dark Brown cardstock 1" wider than the door opening and slightly taller than the opening.

2 Punch the Renaissance Chartres punch in the top area to form a decorative window effect and add a small teardrop of Patina Gold paper for the handle.

3 Attach door to inside of the house.

For the bushes:

1 Cut freeform bushes from Forest Green cardstock with the Victorian-edged scissors.

2 Glue to the sides of the house.

For the flowers:

1 Use the Water Splat punch to create flowers from the Hydrangea Print paper. Punch as many flowers as you desire.

2 Punch on a white section of the Hydrangear Print to make gardenia-looking flowers.

3 Adhere flowers to the bushes.

Completing the project:

1 With craft knife, cut a hole in the back bottom of the house big enough for the cord of the lamp to come through (approximately 2" wide x 1" high).

2 Use the house as a nightlight or a mood lamp.

◆ Mirror Cover

MATERIALS

10" x 27" soft white mat board
Mat knife
8½" x 19½" purchased framed mirror
Emagination Crafts, Inc.™ Craft Punches
  • Impatien Leaf (large)
  • ⅛" Circle (ribbon)
Emagination Crafts, Inc.™
  Bravissimo! Papers (8½" x 11")
  • 2 sheets Dark Blue adhesive-backed
    vellum
  • 2 sheets Light Blue adhesive-
    backed vellum
  • 2 sheets Purple adhesive-backed
    vellum
  • 2 sheets Pink adhesive-backed
    vellum
  • 1 sheet Light Green adhesive-
    backed vellum
  • 1 sheet Dark Green adhesive-
    backed vellum
Fiskars® Mini-Pinking Paper Edgers
E-6000 Glue by Eclectic Products, Inc.
Pencil

Note: Emagination Crafts Vellums come in seasonal color palettes. I used the Spring 2002 colors: Periwinkle, Milk Glass Blue, Spring Lilac, Elfin Magic, and Mint Green. You may substitute different hues from the same color families for your project.

INSTRUCTIONS

1 Copy pattern shape on next page and out of mat board, as shown.

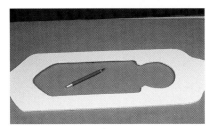

2 With Paper Edgers, cut the leaf shapes out of light green vellum. Use general leaf shape as shown and cut your own variations.

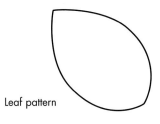

Leaf pattern

3 Remove the backing and add leaf veins. The veins are thin strips of darker green vellum, about 1½" x ⅛". Apply the leaves to the mat board

4 Punch 44 Impatient Leaves out of dark blue vellum, 48 out of light blue vellum, 28 out of pink vellum, and 36 out of purple. Group the darker blue flowers with lighter blue flowers. Group purple and pink flowers together.

> *Tip: I used about 39 flowers to decorate the cover. Each flower requires four Impatien Leaf punches, so if you'd like more flowers, you'll need more punches!*

5 Punch 39 ⅛" circles for the centers of the flowers; you'll need more if you've added more flowers. Use blue circles on the purple flowers and pink circles on the blue flowers.

6 Glue the mat over the mirror.

> *Note: Adjust the mat size to fit the framed mirror that you select.*

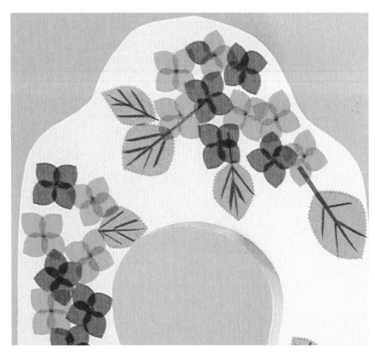

Close-up shots of both the top and bottom of the Mirror Cover show punch placement.

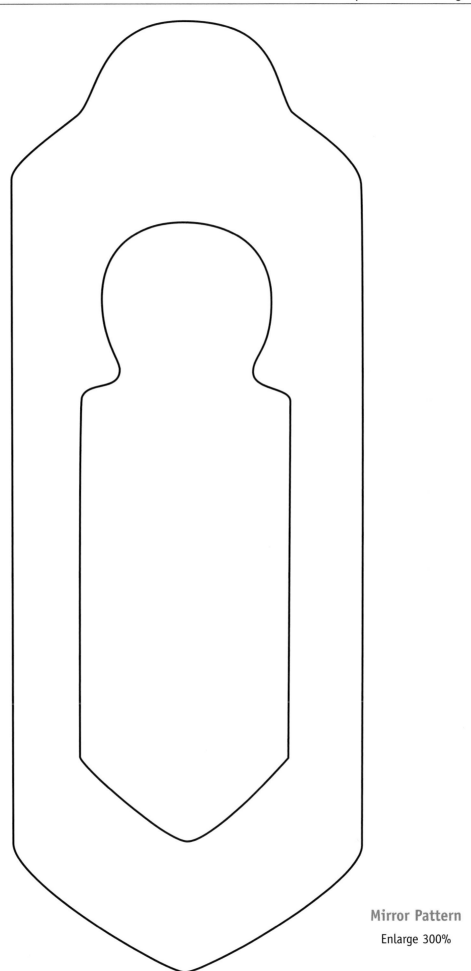

Mirror Pattern

Enlarge 300%

Shoe Pincushion ◆

MATERIALS

Woman's small shoe (I used a size 6½ pump.)
Emagination Crafts, Inc.™ Craft Punch
  • Impatien Leaf (large)
Assorted scrapbooking papers from Anna Griffin, Inc. (8½" x 11")
  • 1 sheet rose variation (yellow and pink)
  • 1 sheet hydrangea variation
  • 1 sheet green
2 sheets assorted true-to-life rose floral papers from NRN Designs (8½" x 11")
10" square cream-colored satin fabric
Cream-colored thread
Needle
Polyester fiberfill
Gloss decoupage medium
DecoArt™ Triple Thick Gloss Glaze
Hot glue gun and glue sticks
Scissors

INSTRUCTIONS

1 Punch approximately 200 Impatien leaves from floral papers. You'll need enough leaves to cover the shoe.

2 Apply the leaves to the shoe with decoupage medium. Start at the front end of the shoe and work towards the back. Overlap the leaves as you go, as shown below, covering all but the sole of the shoe. Overlap the edges of the inner shoe.

3 For the rose ornament, photocopy the Rose Floral Paper using the mirror image option.

4 Glue the photocopy to the back of the Rose Floral Paper, being sure to match the patterns.

5 Cut out the double-sided roses and leaves.

6 Hot glue the base of two leaves together leaving the top ends of the leaves loose.

7 Cut out three roses, one each large, medium, and small.

8 Cut a spiral from the outside of the roses to the center.

9 Manipulate each rose separately to create a cone by pulling the end of the spiral behind the rose and securing it with hot glue.

10 Layer the three roses large to small, glue them together at the center, and apply them to the top of the shoe, as shown below.

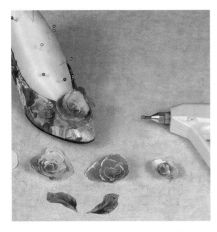

11 Coat the shoe with the Gloss Glaze.

12 Fold the satin fabric square right-sides together.

13 Hand-stitch a ½" seam along the open edge. Leave an opening for turning and stuffing.

14 Turn right-side out and stuff tightly.

15 Sew opening closed.

16 Hot glue inside the shoe.

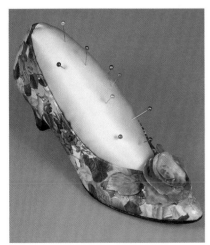

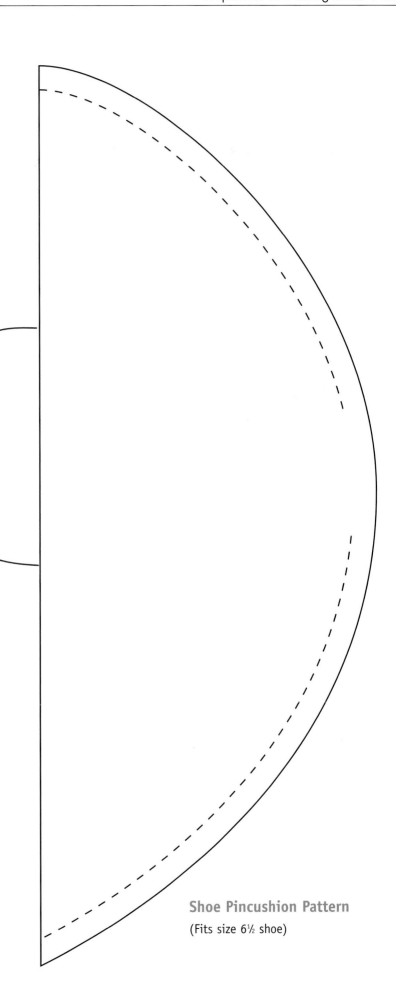

Fold

Shoe Pincushion Pattern
(Fits size 6½ shoe)

Floral Table

MATERIALS

15" x 25" x 15" round accent table by
Walnut Hollow

DecoArt™ Americana® Satins
    Acrylic Enamel
    • 8 oz. jar White Satin
    • 8 oz. jar Light Willow
DecoArt™ Americana® Satins
    Polyurethane Varnish
3 sheets assorted large floral and
    butterfly print papers
    by Anna Griffin (8½" x 11")

1 sheet Calligraphy Paper by
    Papers by Catherine (8½" x 11")
2 photocopies vintage photos,
    postcards, letter, etc.
Scanned pictures of jewelry and small
    purse
Emagination Crafts, Inc.™ Craft Punch
    • Circle (large)
Emagination Crafts, Inc.™
    Bravissimo! Paper (8½" x 11")
    • 2 sheets Patina Copper-Haze
2 sheets Keep A Memory™
    Mounting Adhesive by
    ThermOWeb™ (8½" x 11")
Decoupage medium
Permanent adhesive
Paintbrush

INSTRUCTIONS

1 Paint the table with two coats of White Satin paint. Let dry between coats.

2 Paint one coat of Light Willow over the white paint.

3 Tear the Calligraphy Paper slightly along all four sides to give a deckle look.

4 Decoupage Calligraphy Paper onto the center of the table.

5 Punch 29 circles from Patina Copper paper and apply permanent adhesive.

6 Cut each circle in half.

7 Apply the half-circles around the outside edge of the tabletop. Place the cut edges facing to the outside. Leave ⅛" between circles, as shown.

8 Apply 21 half-circles to the outside edge of the shelf on the table in the same fashion as accomplished on the tabletop.

9 Adhere mounting adhesive to floral papers, photocopies, and color copies. Trim each piece.

10 Apply one flower to the center of the shelf, as shown below.

11 Adhere all of the other pieces to the top of the table.

12 Apply several coats of decoupage medium to the table and shelf.

13 Seal table and shelf with several light coats of varnish. Be sure to let dry completely between coats.

As outlined in step 11, adhere all other pieces to the table top as shown at left.

Room Divider

MATERIALS

3 pieces plywood
  (each cut 16" x 60")
6 silver 1" hinges
DecoArt™ Americana® Satins
  Acrylic Enamel
  • 8 oz. jar Sage Green
DecoArt™ Americana® Satins
  Polyurethane Varnish
40 sheets Keep A Memory™
  Mounting Adhesive Sheets by
  ThermOWeb
Emagination Crafts, Inc.™
  Craft Punches
  • ⅛" Circle (ribbon)
  • ¼" Circle (ribbon)
  • Teardrop (small and large)
Decorative papers (8½" x 11" unless
  otherwise noted)
  • 12 sheets medium to dark solid
  tone-on-tone (for mat)
  • 12 sheets assorted geometric,
  vintage stripes, watercolor florals,
  and feminine tiny florals cut
  10¼" x 7½" (for background)
  • 6 sheets leather-look papers/
  reptile or alligator (for the shoe
  and purse designs)
  • 6 sheets wool, silk, lace, or linen
  look (for hat designs)
  • 3 different real-life flower prints
  (for accents on shoes and hats)
  • 1 sheet metallic paper/gold,
  copper, or silver (for purse clasps
  and handles)
  • Scraps of solid (for eyelets and
  shoe laces)
Border Stickers (enough to cover the
  edge of the mat papers for all 12
  panels)
Paintbrush

A word about decorative papers: I chose papers for this project to give a Victorian look. When you work, choose a theme first. This gives a purpose to the selections you make.

First I chose 12 papers (8½" x 11") to be used as mats for the designs. These were solid papers with texture and tone-on-tone color.

For the backgrounds to apply the designs to, I chose an assortment of lacy-look prints, watercolor florals, Victorian wallpaper looks, small geometric prints, and stripes. These papers give interest to the overall design.

Pull out your stash and look at your scraps and all the papers you bought because you liked them. Look for colors and prints that look like shoes, purses, and hats. Does one look like a purse clasp or a hatband? Choose the papers for your main items: the purse, the hat, and the shoe. Then go back and look for the accents: the flower on the ankle, the hatband, and the purse clasp. Enjoy the process!

INSTRUCTIONS

1 Measure 9¼" from top and bottom and add hinges. Then measure 18" down from the top hinge to add the center hinge.

2 Paint the plywood panels and hinges with Sage Green and let dry. Apply a second coat. Let dry.

3 Apply double-sided adhesive to all papers before cutting.

4 Cut background papers and apply to the mat papers.

5 Trace design patterns, which can be found on pages 88-91, onto your chosen papers. For assistance with paper choice, see pages 93-94.

6 Cut out the designs.

7 Trace accents to chosen accent papers and cut out.

8 Lay out each design. Decide which paper needs to be applied first. For example, the purse bag section is centered and applied to the background first. The upper accent piece is applied next, even with the upper edge and centered. The two teardrop clasps are centered and applied to the upper edge. The hooks for the handles are applied next and then the clasp. The metal-looking strap is applied last.

9 Apply pattern pieces to the plywood frame, as shown on the Placement Patterns, page 92.

10 For the eyelet effect on the boot shoe, punch ⅛" circle and center ¼" circle over ⅛" circle.

11 For the purse handle attachments, use the large teardrop, center the punch over the small teardrop. Use two layer teardrops for the closure of the purse.

12 Apply the border stickers over the finished edges; the sides of each panel first and then tops and bottoms.

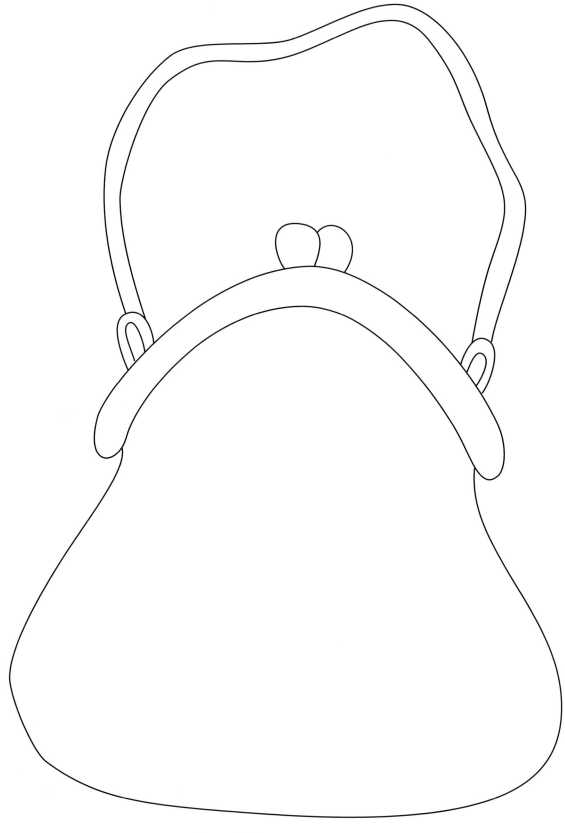

Purse Pattern

Shoe Pattern

Boot Shoe Pattern

Hat Pattern

Hat Pattern

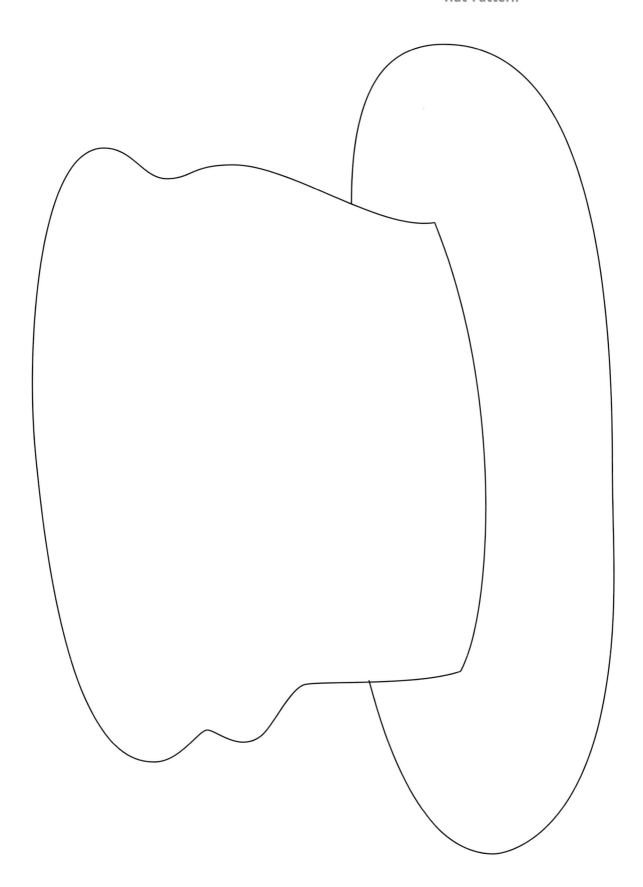

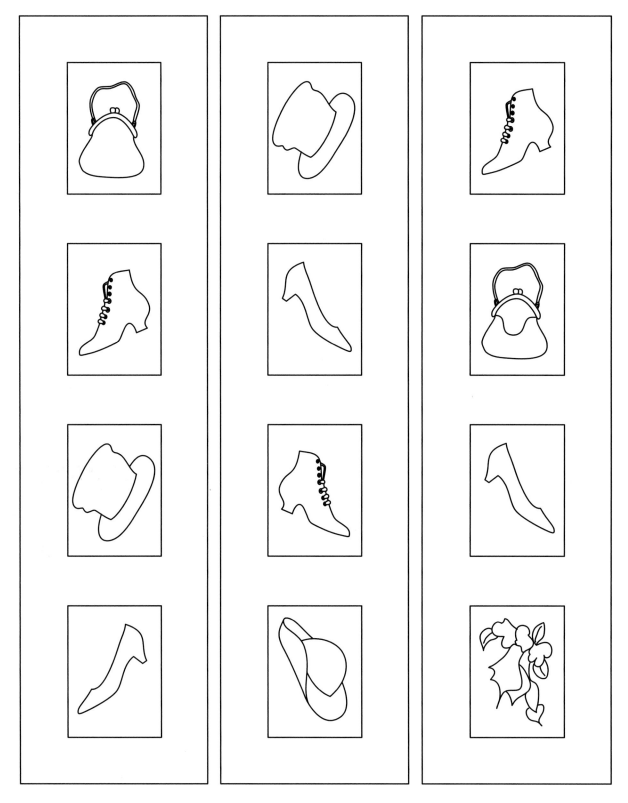

Placement Pattern

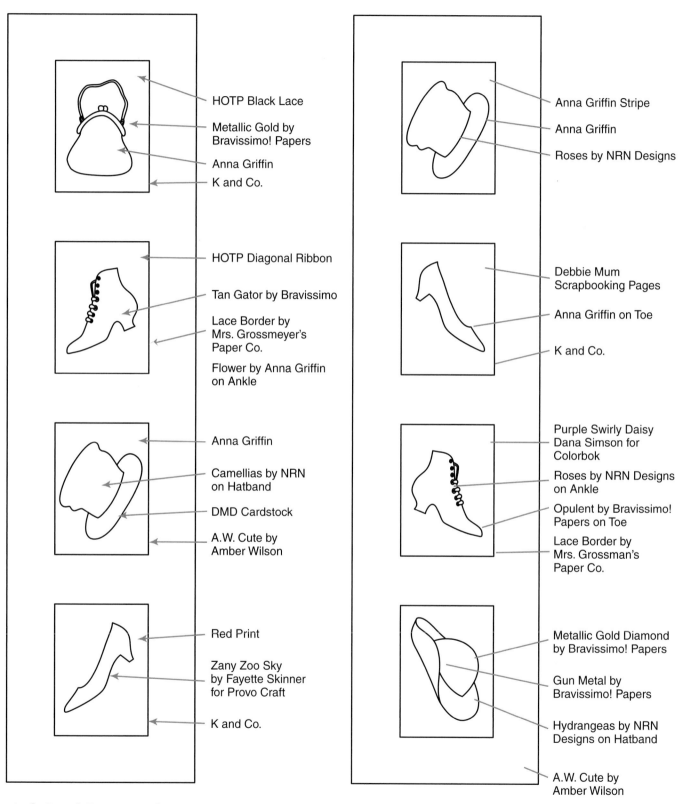

HOTP Black Lace

Metallic Gold by
Bravissimo! Papers

Anna Griffin

K and Co.

HOTP Diagonal Ribbon

Tan Gator by Bravissimo

Lace Border by
Mrs. Grossmeyer's
Paper Co.

Flower by Anna Griffin
on Ankle

Anna Griffin

Camellias by NRN
on Hatband

DMD Cardstock

A.W. Cute by
Amber Wilson

Red Print

Zany Zoo Sky
by Fayette Skinner
for Provo Craft

K and Co.

Anna Griffin Stripe

Anna Griffin

Roses by NRN Designs

Debbie Mum
Scrapbooking Pages

Anna Griffin on Toe

K and Co.

Purple Swirly Daisy
Dana Simson for
Colorbok

Roses by NRN Designs
on Ankle

Opulent by Bravissimo!
Papers on Toe

Lace Border by
Mrs. Grossman's
Paper Co.

Metallic Gold Diamond
by Bravissimo! Papers

Gun Metal by
Bravissimo! Papers

Hydrangeas by NRN
Designs on Hatband

A.W. Cute by
Amber Wilson

Left Panel Frames and Papers

Center Panel Frames and Papers

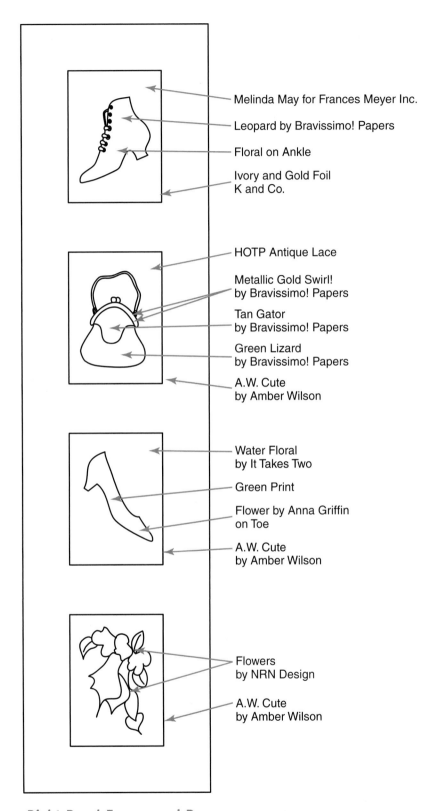

Melinda May for Frances Meyer Inc.

Leopard by Bravissimo! Papers

Floral on Ankle

Ivory and Gold Foil
K and Co.

HOTP Antique Lace

Metallic Gold Swirl!
by Bravissimo! Papers

Tan Gator
by Bravissimo! Papers

Green Lizard
by Bravissimo! Papers

A.W. Cute
by Amber Wilson

Water Floral
by It Takes Two

Green Print

Flower by Anna Griffin
on Toe

A.W. Cute
by Amber Wilson

Flowers
by NRN Design

A.W. Cute
by Amber Wilson

Right Panel Frames and Papers

◆ Chintz Plates

MATERIALS

5 classic wooden plates
by Walnut Hollow
- 10" round,
- 9¾" octagon
- 9½" scallop
- 11½" x 8½" oval
- 9½" square

DecoArt™ Americana® Satins
Acrylic Enamel
- 8 oz. jar White Satin
- 8 oz. jar Soft White
- 8 oz. jar Powder Blue
- 8 oz. jar Powder Pink
- 8 oz. jar Light Willow
DecoArt™ Triple-Thick Gloss Glaze
Floral Patterned Scrapbook Papers
by Frances Meyer (8½" x 11")
- 2 sheets Dogwood
- 2 sheets Pink Flowers
- 2 sheets Blue Flowers
- 2 sheets Pansies
¼-yard Fabric Victorian Prints by
Northcott (blue and red flowers)
Decoupage medium
Paintbrush

INSTRUCTIONS

1 Paint each of the five plates a different color and let dry.

2 Cut out enough individual flowers and leaves to cover each plate.

3 Apply flowers to plates with decoupage medium, covering enough so that just small areas of the plate color show through.

4 Decorate as follows:

- Oval plate—Use Soft White paint and blue flowers from the fabric print. Color copy the fabric prints at 80 percent of the original size. Print several copies. Cut out the flowers and apply to the plates. I placed a large flower in the center of the plate and small and medium flowers around it.

- Scallop plate—Use white paint, along with blue and pink flowers. I alternated the blue and pink flowers around the plate.

- Round plate—Use Powder Pink paint and red flowers from the fabric print. I alternated large and medium flowers around the plate.

- Square plate—Use Light Willow paint and assorted colored pansies. I used assorted colors of pansies in the same size then added tiny pansies around the plate.

- Octagon plate—Use Powder Blue paint and dogwood blossoms. I cut dogwood flowers with leaves and overlapped them around the plate.

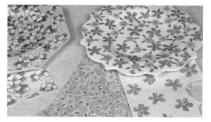

5 Apply several thin coats of decoupage medium over finished plates, being sure to let dry between coats.

6 Hang plates on one wall as a grouping.

Gallery ◆

There are so many more items that you can use to make your own special space truly personal to you. Once again, I really had fun creating projects—more than we can detail—but we've included them here on these Gallery pages to serve as inspiration to you.

The projects shown on this page are: gold floral vase, flower picture on mirror, Washi paper egg, Post-It Note pad, and tall flower box.

Do the possibilities ever end? With all the floral papers available today, it seems there is no end to the possibilities. There is only the limits of your imagination!

The projects shown here are: floral hat stand, large suncatcher, and floral frame.

CHAPTER 8

PROJECTS FOR YOUR BABY'S ROOM

As carefree as pinwheels turning in the breeze.... So describes your little one's days and nights, so why not let the décor of the room where he or she spends the majority of those days and nights reflect that pleasant image?

Use a favorite poem or song as your decorating inspiration for this precious room. Lettering stencils and markers make it easy for you to transfer sentiment to walls and furniture.

Simple painting techniques and quilt block designs accent a delightful retreat for you and your baby. Choose your palette and give a splash of color with the decorative papers turned into quilt designs.

Just imagining the pinwheels gently spinning will give you and your child peace and happiness because as Emily Dickinson once wrote: "Exhilaration is the breeze that lifts us from the ground."

Cloud Wall Décor ◆

MATERIALS

For cloud background
White flat paint (enough to cover walls)
Paint roller and pan
16 oz. container Ultra Blue Dry Tempera
    Paint by Palmer Paint Products
Sea sponge
12" x 12" scrap cardstock piece
    (for template)
Lettering template – Giggly,
    The Crafter's Workshop (TCW17)
Splash Zig Writer Pen
Krylon Workable Fixative
Paper plates
Newspaper

> Note: This painting
> technique can be applied
> to the entire room, or just
> one wall.

INSTRUCTIONS

1 Tape newspaper around the room's baseboard. This will mask for painting and keep the dust from the "chalking" off the carpet.
2 Paint the room flat white and let dry.

> Tip: After applying clouds and poem, you could paint the lower part of the white wall another coat of semi-gloss to allow for easy cleaning.

3 Cut out a large cloud template from cardstock. Use the pattern on the next page and enlarge 200 percent, or draw your own.
4 To accomplish the "chalking" technique for the clouds, begin by pouring a ¼ cup of Ultra Blue dry tempera paint onto a paper plate.
5 Starting in a top left corner of the room, hold the cloud template where you'd like the first cloud to appear and dip the dry sponge into the tempera paint. With a slight rubbing motion, follow the top line of the cloud—not all the way around. You may need to dip sponge several times.
6 Wipe off the cloud template with a soft cloth and continue onto the next cloud by overlap-

ping the first "chalked" cloud and again apply the tempera paint around the cloud template. Repeat this process across and down the wall as desired.

Tip: Any dry paint that goes where you don't want it can be removed with a white art eraser when chalking is finished.

7 With Splash Zig Writer Pen and letter template, stencil the following poem onto the wall all along the inside cloud edges.

> *Exhilaration is the Breeze*
> *That lifts us from the ground,*
> *And leaves us in another place*
> *Whose statement is not found;*
> *Returns us not, but after time*
> *We soberly descend,*
> *A little newer for the term*
> *Upon enchanted ground.*
> *—Emily Dickinson*

8 Seal the "chalking" with Krylon Fixative. Open all the windows in the room and close the doors for ventilation. Start in the upper left corner and spray the fixative on, holding the can 12" to 18" inches from the wall.

Enlarge 200%

Cloud Template

Wall Pinwheels ◆━━━━━━━━━━━

MATERIALS

Enough to make one pinwheel:

2 sheets print paper
2 sheets solid paper (coordinating with prints)
Permanent adhesive
³⁄₁₆" hole punch
8 Emagination Crafts, Inc.™ eyelets
Emagination Crafts, Inc.™ eyelet setter
Emagination Crafts, Inc.™ Craft Punches
  • Flower or Circle (large)

Hammer
Craft mat
8½" x 11" cardboard piece (for template)
2 drinking straws (cut into ½" pieces)
36" x ½" square balsa wood stick by
    Midwest Products (cut into 18" lengths)
1½"-long wood screw (#6)
2 foam double-sided ½"adhesive dots
Pencil
Scissors or rotary cutter

Note: The following method is the way that all pinwheels will be made for the Baby's Room. The only difference will be the size of the square that you start with.

INSTRUCTIONS

For the pinwheel squares:

1 Cut print and solid papers into 8½" squares. You will need one solid and one print square for each pinwheel.

2 Apply permanent adhesive to the back of the print square.

3 Peel the paper off the back of the square.

4 Carefully line up the adhesive-backed print square and apply to the back of the desired solid square. Rub firmly to make a nice bond. If any of the edges are not matching, just trim with scissors.

5 Repeat steps 2 through 4 for all squares.

For the pinwheel template:

1 Cut an 8½" square from cardboard to create a template.

2 Fold the cardboard template square into fourths and using the point of a pencil, make a small hole in the center.

3 With a pencil, draw a line from corner to corner.

4 Punch a ³⁄₁₆" hole in each quadrant, as indicated in Figure 1 below. Use a smaller hole when making a smaller pinwheel.

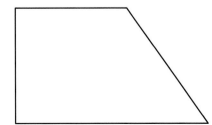

Figure 1

Finishing the pinwheels:

1 Lay the template on one of the double-sided squares.

2 With a pencil, mark the hole in the center and the corner holes. With your ³⁄₁₆" eyelet punch, hammer, and mat, and punch an eyelet hole in each of the corners and the center of the double-sided square.

3 Repeat steps 1 and 2 above for all double-sided squares.

4 Cut 3" in from each corner of the double-sided square to make the pinwheel blades, as shown.

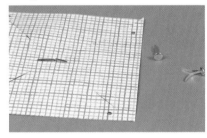

5 Using a contrasting print paper, make the pinwheel center by punching a ³⁄₁₆" hole about 1" in from the edge of the paper.

6 Punch a circle or flower by turning the punch over and centering on the small hole and punch.

7 Starting with one of the corners, bring the punched eyelet hole into the center, matching it up with the center eyelet hole. Repeat around until all corners are in the center.

8 Place the circle or flower on top, matching the hole.

9 Apply the eyelet, securing it on the backside. If you use an eyelet, the pinwheel will have the ability to turn when attached to the stick. If you choose to use a brad instead, it will be stationary.

Attaching the pinwheel:

1 To attach the pinwheel to the sticks, use a ¹⁄₁₆" drill bit and drill a hole 1" from the end of each stick. Repeat for each pinwheel you plan to attach to the wall. (This will keep the screw from splitting the wood.)

2 Insert the screw through the eyelet opening, followed by a ½" piece of drinking straw, and screw into the wood stick where the small hole was drilled, as shown.

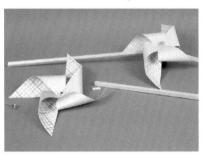

3 Place the pinwheel where desired on the wall, and screw into the wall. Because of the light nature of this pinwheel, you do not need to attach it to a stud.

4 Apply two double-side sticky dots to the stick to hold it onto the wall.

Pinwheel Lamp ◆

MATERIALS

Purchased white lamp and shade
Letter template – Giggly Mini,
   The Crafter's Workshop
DecoArt™ Americana® Acrylic Paint
  • 2 oz. bottle Country Blue
Sea sponge
6 assorted 2"-square print paper scraps
6 assorted 2"-square solid paper scraps
Permanent adhesive
6 tiny brads
1 sheet kraft-colored cardstock from
   DMD Paper Reflections® (8½" x 11")
6 Sticky Dots® double-sided adhesive
   by ThermOWeb

INSTRUCTIONS

1 Using a very dry sponge with little paint, sponge paint around the lampshade and let dry.

2 Using Giggly template and Splash Zig Writer Pen, stencil part of the wall poem (page 101) around the lower edge of the shade.

3 Make tiny pinwheel, following the same method as used for the Wall Pinwheels project (page 103), except starting with 2" squares.

Note: The materials list suggests six pinwheels will be necessary to border your lampshade; however, you may measure around the top edge of your shade and plan accordingly for enough 2" pinwheels to border sufficiently.

4 Use tiny brads to secure each pinwheel center.

5 Adhere each pinwheel to the lamp along the top edge with Sticky Dots.

6 Cut kraft cardstock into 3" x ¼" strips. Apply adhesive and attach under each pinwheel.

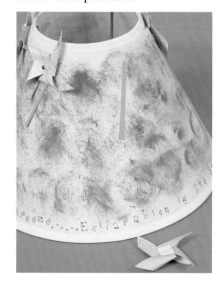

Pinwheel Table

MATERIALS

23" x 23" x 16" unfinished oval side table by Walnut Hollow

DecoArt™ Americana® Acrylic Paint
- 2 oz. bottle White
- 2 oz. bottle Country Blue
- 2 oz. bottle Arbor Green
- 2 oz. bottle Lemon Yellow

DecoArt™ Americana® Polyurethane Varnish

6 assorted 2"-square print or solid paper scraps

6 assorted 3"-square print or solid paper scraps

1 sheet kraft-colored cardstock from DMD Paper Reflections (8½" x 11")

Sea sponge

Lettering template – Giggly, The Crafter's Workshop (TCW17)

Splash Zig Writer Pen
Decoupage medium
Permanent adhesive
Painters' tape
Paintbrush

INSTRUCTIONS

1 Paint the entire table. I used white on the tabletop, blue on the legs, and yellow on the shelves and drawer. Let dry.

2 Mark off 2" border around tabletop with painters' tape.

3 Sponge inside the border lightly with Country Blue paint.

4 Use the lettering stencil to write part of poem from page 101 around the border. You may need to resize patterns to fit your table.

5 For the paper patchwork pinwheels on the tabletop, apply permanent adhesive to all papers.

6 Cut two 3" squares and two 2" squares in coordinating papers for each pinwheel.

7 Cut each square in half diagonally to form triangle pieces. You will have four triangles from the two 3" squares and four from the 2" squares.

8 Then cut each of the triangles down the center to form smaller triangles, as shown in Figure 1. Do the same with the triangles from the 2" square.

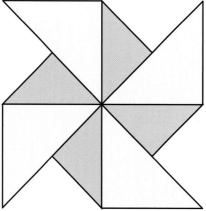

Figure 1

9 Assemble the pinwheels on top of the table, alternating four larger triangles with four smaller triangles in a contrasting print, as shown in the following photos.

10 Cut kraft cardstock into three strips approximately ¼" x 2" and apply to tabletop underneath pinwheels to form the pinwheel sticks.

11 Apply pinwheels to the table. Apply decoupage to the top of the pinwheel. You may have some wrinkling. Smooth out the wrinkles with your fingers as much as you can.

12 Apply varnish to the entire table.

◆ Pinwheel Frame

MATERIALS

8" x 10" wooden frame
  by Maple Lane Press
Coordinating prints papers (I used prints
  from Paper Patch®, Doodlebug
  Design Inc.™ and Colorbok.)
  • 2 sheets solids (8½" x 11")
  • 2 sheets prints (8½" x 11")
Permanent adhesive
Emagination Crafts, Inc.™ Craft Punches
  • Square (super jumbo and super
    giant)
Chevron (super giant)
4 Emagination Crafts, Inc.™ ⅛" eyelets
Emagination Crafts, Inc.™ eyelet setter
Tacky glue
4 double-sided ½" adhesive dots

INSTRUCTIONS

1 Apply permanent adhesive to backs of papers.

2 Punch four super jumbo squares from solid papers. These are corner squares.

3 Punch 16 chevrons: 10 from one color and six from a contrast print.

4 Punch four super giant squares in paper of your choice.

5 Cut the four super giant squares in half diagonally to make triangles.

6 Punch two super giant squares for the pinwheels in the corners in paper of your choice.

7 Cut the two super giant pinwheel squares in half lengthwise and cut off the corner of one end as shown in Figure 1.

Figure 1

8 Assemble punched pieces on frame, as follows: apply squares in the corners and chevrons between corners, alternating colors with all facing the same direction. See photo at right for punch placement.

9 Place adhesive dot in center of corner squares. Assemble pinwheels on the double-sided adhesive dots.

10 Flatten eyelets with setting tool and adhere them with tacky glue to center of the four corner pinwheels, as shown at right.

Pinwheel Album Cover ◆

MATERIALS

Fabric-covered album
Decorative papers (8½" x 11")
  • 1 sheet solid blue paper
  • 1 sheet background paper
    (if not using computer)
June Tailor Iron-On Inkjet Printable
  Fabric Sheet
Epson printer
Scanner
Four color copies of a photograph
  or program
Applicable computer program (Print
  Shop, Publisher, MGI Photosuite,
  Microsoft Photo Editor, etc.)
Lettering stickers or stencil
  (if not using computer)
Tacky glue (if not using fusible transfer)

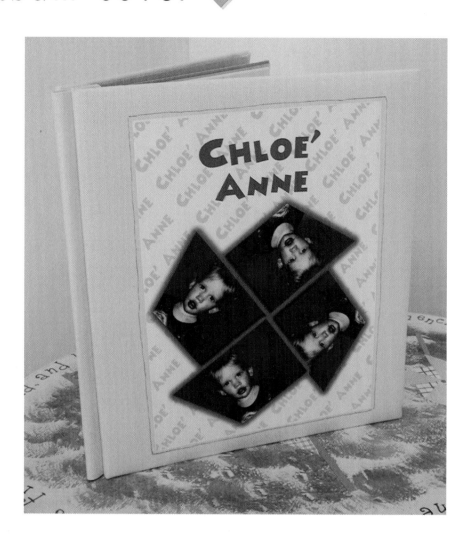

INSTRUCTIONS

1 Crop photographs to a pinwheel blade shape, as shown in Figure 1. You can scan your picture into an editing program such as those listed in the materials list.

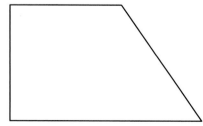

Figure 1

2 Copy, paste, and rotate image to create pinwheel, as shown in the following photo.

3 Add a border to pinwheel by cutting pattern ¼" larger than photo and applying cropped photo to center of solid blue paper.

4 Add background and title. Use your computer to print a background and title or use stencils and decorative paper. Print out design onto Inkjet Printable Fabric Sheet.

5 Iron fabric sheet on to the front of the album following package instructions, or use tacky glue to glue onto album if you are not working with a fusible transfer.

◆ Pinwheel Toy Chest

MATERIALS

30" x 21" x 10" Storage Bench
  by Walnut Hollow

DecoArt™ Americana® Satins
  Acrylic Enamel
  • 8 oz. jar White
  • 8 oz. jar Arbor Green
  • 8 oz. jar Country Blue
DecoArt™ Americana® Polyurethane
  Varnish
Sea sponge
Coordinating print papers (8½" x 11")
  • 3 sheets different plaid
  • 3 sheets different polka-dots
  • 3 sheets different solids
  • 3 sheets same background solid

Permanent adhesive
Satin decoupage medium
Scissors
Cutting mat
Rotary cutter
Paintbrush

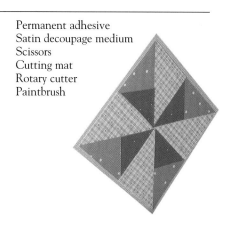

INSTRUCTIONS

1 Paint toy chest white. Accent areas with Arbor Green and Country Blue as desired. Let dry.

2 Sponge top of chest with Country Blue paint, as shown below, and let dry.

3 To create the quilt square effect on the front of the toy chest, you will need to cut the following for each square:

- one 6½" square
- one 6" square
- two 3" squares
- two 2" squares

4 Apply double-sided adhesive to the back of the squares.

5 Cut the 2" and 3" squares diagonally, making four triangles each.

6 Using the 6½" square as a base, center and apply the 6" square on top, as shown in next photo.

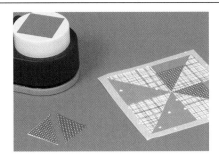

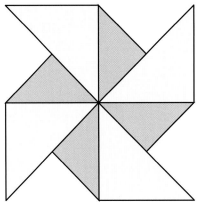

6 Apply the large triangle, as shown in Figure 1 below, and repeat around square.

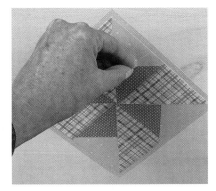

Figure 1

7 Apply small triangles as shown and repeat around square.

8 Apply pinwheels to the front of the chest, as shown in the following two photos.

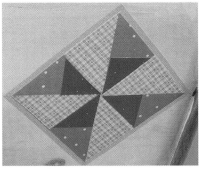

9 Apply decoupage over the quilt square. Because of the thin nature of the paper, you may have some wrinkling. Smooth out with fingers as much as you can.

10 Apply a coat of decoupage medium on the entire front of toy chest.

11 Apply varnish to the entire chest.

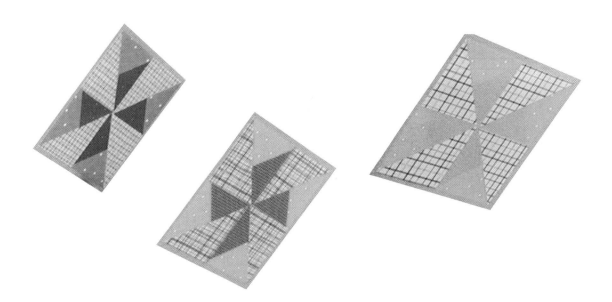

Pinwheel Rocking Chair

MATERIALS

Flea market-purchased rocking chair
DecoArt™ Americana® Satins
   Acrylic Enamel
  • 8 oz. jar Country Blue
  • 8 oz. jar Arbor Green
  • 8 oz. jar Lemon Yellow
  • 8 oz. jar White
DecoArt™ Americana® Polyurethane
   Varnish
Sea sponge
Lettering template – Giggly,
   The Crafter's Workshop (TCW17)
Splash Zig Writer Pen
Painters' tape
Paintbrush

Note: Since rocking chairs are all different, make changes to your layout to fit your rocker.

INSTRUCTIONS

1 Paint entire rocking chair white and let dry.

2 Accent other areas of the rocker with green, blue, and yellow paints as desired and let dry.

3 With painters' tape, mark off a two-inch border on the edge of the chair back.

4 Sponge the center area with Country Blue paint to create a cloud effect and let dry.

5 Remove the painters' tape and use the lettering template to add a verse of the poem on page 101 in the border area.

6 Add a paper patchwork pinwheel to the center of the sponged area. Refer to the instructions in the Pinwheel Table project (page 106) to guide you.

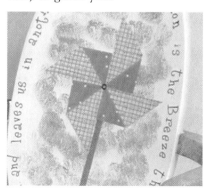

7 Apply a coat of decoupage medium to the chair back. Let dry. Several coats of medium may be needed. The surface will be done when it feels smooth.

8 Apply varnish to seal.

CHAPTER 9

PROJECTS FOR YOUR GIRL'S ROOM

It's time to get a little funky with an explosion of color. Bright yellow, lime green, and hot pink come together to make this room creative and fun—just like your daughter!

These projects have personality plus. And that personality shines through as you complete the projects to match your child's talents, hobbies, and interests. The beauty is that no two people making these projects will come up with rooms looking exactly the same; they adapt to showcase the special aspects of your child.

I fell in love with the paper dolls available in scrapbooking stores. Let the girl in your life choose the clothes and accessories for these paper dolls so that she's happy with the end results.

Don't forget to use her favorite photos of friends and pets to accent each item. Think about how your child and her friends will feel when they find themselves stars of their own room décor.

Lamp

MATERIALS

White candlestick lamp
10"-high square lampshade with 4" top
    and 8" bottom
Approximately 40 white key tags
Emagination Crafts, Inc.™ Craft Punches
  • Circle (large)
  • ⅛" Hole (ribbon)
  • Allegro (jumbo)
⅛" eyelet hole punch and hammer
Punch Bunch™ Craft Punches
  • Large Swirl
  • Giant Swirl
40 assorted color Dot Stickers
    by Mrs. Grossman's
Cardstock by DMD Paper Reflections®
    (8½" x 11")
  • 1 sheet Fushcia
  • 1 sheet Granny Apple Green
  • 1 sheet Bright Purple
  • 1 sheet Orange
  • 1 sheet Purple
  • 1 sheet Yellow
Tacky glue
Permanent adhesive

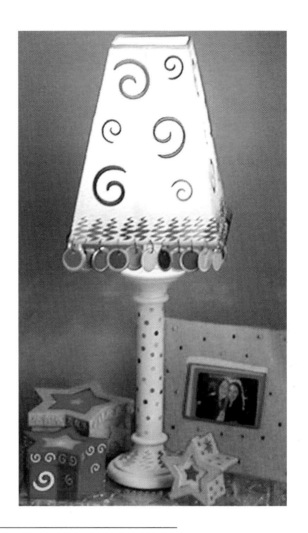

INSTRUCTIONS

1 Apply the colored stickers dots randomly to the midsection of the lamp.

2 Punch eight Allegro punches from each color of cardstock (48 punches total).

3 Apply Allegro punches to lamp base, as shown below.

4 Punch one hole every inch around the bottom edge of the lampshade using the eyelet hole punch, as shown in the next photo.

5 Punch two large circles of each color of cardstock (12 punches total).

6 Punch ⅛" holes in the top of each circle.

7 Temporarily remove the metal ring from the key tags.

8 Glue one matching colored circle to each side of tag.

9 Put the metal rings back into the key tags and attach the tags to the holes in lampshade.

10 Adhere assorted colors of Allegro punches on the lampshade between and above the key tags.

11 Punch 12 giant swirls and 12 large swirls from assorted cardstock colors and adhere three of each size punch on each side of the lampshade.

Floor Cloth

MATERIALS

30" round Kreative Kraft® Precoated
   Decorative Surface by Kunin Felt
DecoArt™ Americana® Acrylic Paint
  • 2 oz. bottle White
  • 2 oz. bottle Salem Blue
  • 2 oz. bottle Indian Turquoise
Zig® Memory Systems Calligraphy Pens
  • Fuchsia
  • Kiwi
  • Orchid
  • Summer Sun
  • Island Coral
  • Clover
  • Candy Pink
Emagination Crafts Inc.™ Craft Punches
  • Allegro (super giant)
  • Water Splat (super jumbo)
  • Circle (large)
Punch Bunch™ Craft Punches
  • Large Swirl
  • Giant Circle
Hearts die-cut
Cardstock by DMD Paper Reflections®
  (8½" x 11")
  • 1 sheet Fushcia
  • 1 sheet Granny Apple Green
  • 1 sheet Grape
  • 1 sheet Hot Pink
  • 1 sheet Orange
  • 1 sheet Neon Yellow
Permanent adhesive
7 assorted color Dot Stickers
  by Mrs. Grossman's
5 Paperkins® paper dolls by EK Success
  (your choice)
Sea sponge

INSTRUCTIONS

1 Mark a 2¾" border around edge of floor cloth.
2 Use calligraphy markers (5mm point) to draw 2¾" long fringe around the edge, as shown. Be sure to draw lines that look like fringe in motion, not just straight lines, as shown.

3 Paint the center portion of the floor cloth by sponging lightly first Salem Blue and then Indian Turquoise paint.
4 Adhere all five of the paper dolls around the edge of the turquoise-blue center portion of floor cloth. Evenly space the paper dolls with feet toward the fringe.

5 Punch as follows: five large swirls, four small swirls, six Water Splats, and four Allegros.
6 Adhere the punched shapes and seven dot stickers.
7 Apply many light coats of varnish to seal the rug. Be sure to let dry between coats.

Star Boxes

MATERIALS

3 papier-mâché star boxes with star inserts in the lids by MB Glick
- 2" x 4"
- 3" x 5"
- 3½" x 6"

DecoArt™ Americana® Acrylic Paint
- 2 oz. bottle Yellow Light
- 2 oz. bottle Tangelo Orange
- 2 oz. bottle Indian Turquoise

DecoArt™ Americana® Satin Polyurethane Varnish

Cardstock by DMD Paper Reflections® (8½" x 11")
- 1 sheet Sunburst
- 1 sheet Emerald
- 1 sheet Orange
- 1 sheet Bright Purple

Emagination Craft, Inc.™ Craft Punches
- ½" Circle (ribbon)
- Primitive Star (small, large, and super jumbo)
- Spiral (small)
- Water Splat (large)

Large Swirl Craft Punch by Punch Bunch™

Permanent adhesive

Paintbrush

INSTRUCTIONS

1 Paint the small box yellow, medium box orange, and largest box turquoise and let dry.

<u>For the small box (2½" x 4"):</u>
1 Cover the star insert with the Emerald cardstock.
2 Apply a large purple Primitive Star punch in the center.
3 Punch approximately 20 purple ¼" circles and apply around the sides of the box top.
4 Punch six purple large Water Splats and approximately 18 purple ¼" circles and apply around the sides of the box.

<u>For the medium box (3" x 5"):</u>
1 Cover the star insert with Sunburst cardstock.
2 Punch about 20 large Emerald Primitive Star and apply to the center.
3 Punch about 20 small Emerald spirals and apply to the sides of the box top.
4 Punch five small Emerald spirals and five large Emerald swirls and apply to sides of box.

<u>For the large box (3½" x 6"):</u>
1 Cover the star insert with orange cardstock.

2 Apply a large Sunburst Primitive Star to the center.
3 Punch 30 small Sunburst stars and apply to the sides of the box top.
4 Punch five small Sunburst stars and five super jumbo Sunburst stars and apply to the sides of the box.

5 Apply varnish to all three boxes.

Eyelet Frame

MATERIALS

8" x 10" acrylic frame
Cardstock by DMD Paper Reflections®
   (8½" x 11")
  • 1 sheet Orange
  • 1 sheet Bright Purple
  • 1 sheet Hot Pink
  • 1 sheet Parakeet Blue
  • 1 sheet Emerald
  • 1 sheet Sunburst
30 Emagination Crafts, Inc.™ eyelets in
   assorted colors
Eyelet setter
Emagination Crafts, Inc.™ Craft Punch
  • ½" Circle
Hammer
Bead and glass glue
Fiskars® Rectangular Shape Template
Fiskars® Shape Cutter
Keep A Memory™ Mounting Adhesive
   Tape by ThermOWeb
Craft knife

INSTRUCTIONS

1 Using the shape cutter and rectangular shape template, cut a rectangle (approximately ½" to ¾" smaller than photo size) in the center of each piece of cardstock. Eyeball the center, don't measure it.

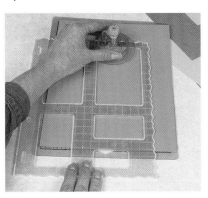

2 Stack paper up with the rectangles staggered so that all of the colors show in the cutout section. With a craft knife, trim the stack to measure 8" x 10", as shown below.

3 Use the mounting tape to lightly secure the sheets together.
4 Punch 30 holes.
5 Add eyelets to holes, as shown.

6 Glue to the acrylic frame.

Decorative Tassel ◆

MATERIALS

Wooden tassel top by Toner Plastics
Cardstock by DMD Paper Reflections®
(8½" x 11")
- 1 sheet Orange
- 1 sheet Bright Purple
- 1 sheet Hot Pink
- 1 sheet Aqua
- 1 sheet Sunburst

6 yards each of assorted ribbons in assorted widths to match cardstock colors
24" long x 1½" wide blue sheer ribbon (for hanging)
Emagination Crafts Inc.™ Craft Punches
- Spiral (small)

Emagination Crafts, Inc.™
The Edge Wave Scissors
Large Swirl Craft Punch
by Punch Bunch™
Fiskars® Wavy Crimper
18" Trimtations™ Designer Accents bead trim from Expo International
Hot glue gun and glue sticks
Permanent adhesive
DecoArt™ Americana™ Satins
Acrylic Enamel
- 8 oz. Yellow Green

DecoArt™ Americana™ Polyurethane
Varnish
2 rubber bands
Paintbrush
Xyron machine or permanent adhesive

INSTRUCTIONS

1 Paint tassel top with Yellow Green paint and let dry.

2 Punch two to three swirls and two to three spirals from all cardstocks colors (10 to 15 total swirl punches and 10 to 15 total spiral punches).

3 Run punches through Xyron machine, as shown below.

4 Apply punches to tassel top.

5 Apply several coats of varnish to tassel top. Let dry between coats.

6 Cut paper into 11" strips with wave scissors and run each strip through the crimper, as shown.

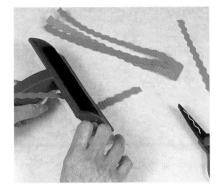

7 Cut ribbons into 24" lengths.

8 Organize the paper strips into a group. While holding the top end with one hand and keeping the tops even, wrap a rubber band tightly around the top edge of the strips.

9 Fold ribbons in half and arrange over the paper strips and apply a second rubber band over the top.

10 Hot glue a double row of beaded fringe inside the bottom edge of the tassel top, as shown below.

11 Push the ends of the sheer blue ribbon into the hole on the end of the tassel top, as shown below.

12 Divide the tassel in half, as shown below, and tie the ends of the ribbon in a double knot. Cut off the excess and pull the ribbon so that the tassel goes up into the tassel top.

Paper Roll Pillow

MATERIALS

21" x 31" Handmade Cat Paper
   by The Lacey Paper Co.
1 piece plain paper
Bolster pillow
Emagination Crafts, Inc.™
   Twistart™ Paper Yarn
   • 1 skein Tangerine Dream
   • 1 skein Snow White
2 rubber bands
20" x 22" heavy fusible interfacing
Hot glue gun and glue sticks
Iron

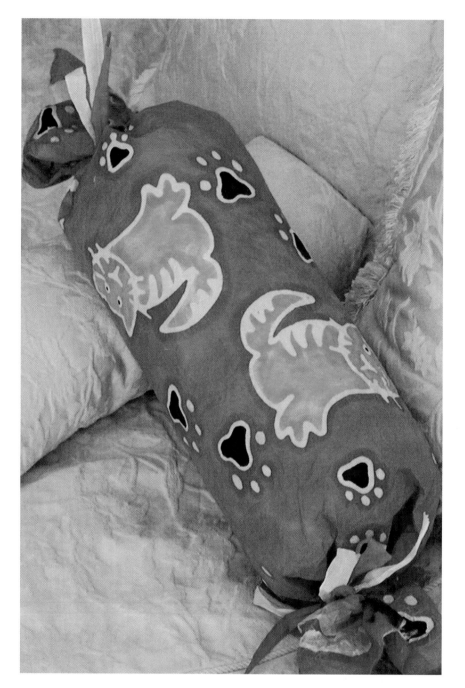

INSTRUCTIONS

1 Ball up Handmade Cat Paper several times to soften the fibers.
2 Using a plain piece of paper as a cover sheet, iron the Handmade Cat Paper.
3 Center and fuse the interfacing to the wrong side of the Handmade Cat Paper.
4 Roll the interfaced cat paper into a tube, overlapping the edges, and glue with the glue gun.
5 Use the rubber bands to secure the ends of the paper tube.
6 Open up paper yarn and cut both skeins in half.
7 Split skeins and mix colors, making one group with half of both colors.
8 Using one mixed skein, wrap the centers of the yarn around one end and tie a knot and then a bow.
9 Do the same with the other mixed skein on the other end. Trim ends and fluff out pillow ends.

◆ Square Flower Pillow

MATERIALS

12" square pillow (or any size larger than your photo)
8½" x 11" Colorfast Fusible Inkjet Printable Fabric by June Tailor Inc.
8" x 10" photo (or any photo smaller than your pillow)
2 large Foam Flowers by Creative Hands Fibre Craft
4 to 6 assorted size/color buttons
Embroidery floss (to match buttons)
Oval stencil
Computer, printer, and applicable software
Iron
Sewing thread to match pillow
Sewing needle

Pillow variations abound, as shown in the three examples above. Try using photos of friends, pets, or even vacation spots. Scan them with your computer and print each onto Ink Jet Printable fabric.

INSTRUCTIONS

1 Print photo on fabric, following manufacturer's instructions.

2 Open seam on pillow and remove the stuffing inside.

3 Use a large oval stencil to center and mark the fabric photo.
4 Fuse the oval to the front of the pillow.
5 Place the foam flowers at a diagonal on top and bottom of oval.
6 Position the buttons over the foam flowers and use a six-strand embroidery floss to sew the buttons in place.
7 Add additional buttons as you'd like for decorations.
8 Restuff pillow and sew seam closed with thread.

Bookshelf

MATERIALS

22½" wide x 47½" high and 8" deep corner shelf by Walnut Hollow

DecoArt™ Americana® Satins Acrylic Enamel
• 8 oz. bottle White Satin
DecoArt™ Triple Thick Gloss Glaze
12 medium Funky Flower Background Design Stickers by Provo Craft
4 large Funky Flower Background Design Stickers by Provo Craft

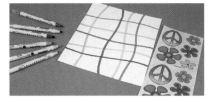

Zig® Memory System Calligraphy Pens
• Orchid
• Summer Sun
• Fuchsia
• Island Coral
• Kiwi
• Candy Pink
Paintbrush

INSTRUCTIONS

1 Paint shelf with White Satin paint and let dry.

2 In random order, choose a 5.0 calligraphy marker and draw a wavy line the height of the bookshelf.

3 Continue to draw lines 2" to 4" apart, alternating all six marker colors. Don't worry about patterns or if the same number of lines appear in each section.

4 Repeat the same process when drawing horizontal lines on the bookshelf. A funky plaid pattern emerges.

5 Apply one large flower sticker and three medium flower stickers randomly to each section.

6 Apply many light coats of varnish over bookshelf. Be sure to let dry between coats.

Glass Vase

MATERIALS

10"-high clear glass vase
14" clear plastic ½"-wide tubing
Assorted paper scraps in prints and solids
Emagination Crafts, Inc.™ Craft Punches
  • Circle (super jumbo)
  • Square (super jumbo)
  • Allegro (super giant)
  • Primitive Star (super jumbo)
  • Flower (small and large)
  • Water Splat (large)
Large Swirl Punch by Punch Bunch™
Permanent adhesive
DecoArt™ Americana® Satins
  Acrylic Enamel
  • 8 oz. jar Soft White
Paintbrush
Xyron machine
Craft knife
Rubbing alcohol

INSTRUCTIONS

1 Clean the vase thoroughly with rubbing alcohol and let dry.
2 Punch assorted solid paper shapes in your choice of colors and run through the Xyron.
3 With permanent adhesive, attach the shapes to the inside of the vase. Rub out any bubbles.

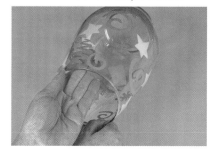

4 Run print paper scraps through the Xyron machine face down.

5 Tear the print papers into random pieces and adhere to the inside of the vase.
6 Cover any holes in the paper surface with solid paper with adhesive on it.

7 Paint the inside of the vase with Soft White paint and let dry.
8 Cut a slit down on inside of the plastic tube and insert the print paper into the tube, as shown.

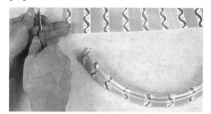

9 Add tube to the top of the vase to finish the upper edge. Trim to fit.

Styrofoam Head Photo Holder

MATERIALS

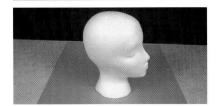

Styrofoam head (beauty supply store type)
Old ceramic soup bowl (large enough to set head on to serve as the base)
Paper towels
4 oz. wheat paste
DecoArt™ Americana® Acrylic Paint
  • 4 oz. (2 bottles) Yellow Green
DecoArt™ Americana® Polyurethane Varnish
2 packages yellow/orange Toobs™- Interconnecting flexible tubes in four sizes
7 alligator clips (hardware store)
4 yards 18-gauge wire
4 yards 10-gauge wire
1 package Creative Hands™ Foam Flowers by FiberCraft®
Provo Craft® Scrapbook "Biggies" stickers
2 packages Purple Buds designed by Cara Bradshaw
2 packages Plaid Flowers designed by Jill Webster
Emagination Crafts, Inc.™ Craft Punches
  • Sun (super giant)
  • ⅛" hole punch
6" square Black Cardstock by DMD Paper Reflections®
Tacky glue
Handful of rocks
Cardboard scrap
Paintbrush

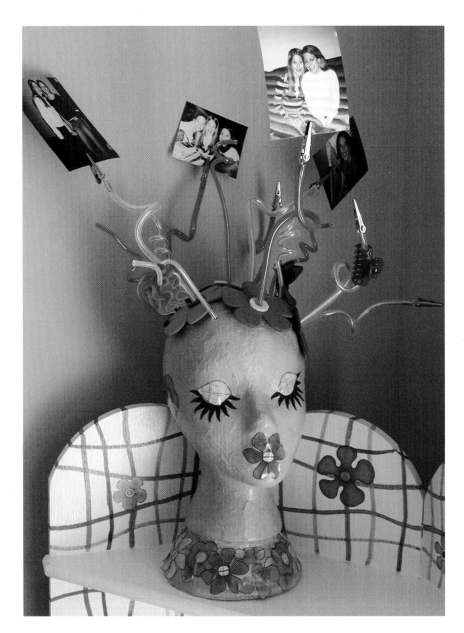

INSTRUCTIONS

1 Turn the soup bowl upside-down on flat surface and glue the Styrofoam head base to the bowl. Let dry.

2 Fill the bowl with rocks. Glue the cardboard over the bowl opening. Let dry. This weighs the base of the head down so that it will not turn over.

3 Tear paper towel into pieces approximately 1½" square. You will need enough pieces to cover the head two times.

4 Dip pieces into wheat paste and smooth onto head and bowl, covering head and base completely, twice. Let dry.

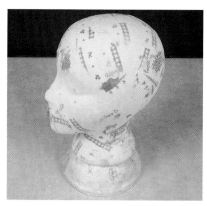

5 Paint head and base with Yellow Green paint and let dry.

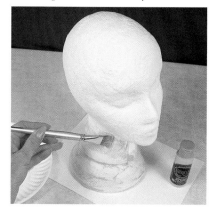

6 Apply varnish and let dry.

7 Punch ⅛" circle in the center of each of seven Foam Flowers and flower centers.

8 Glue each flower and its center to the top of the head.

9 Cut both the 10- and 18-gauge wires into 12" pieces. You will end up with 12 pieces of each gauge, or 24 pieces total.

10 Top seven of the 10-gauge wires with alligator clips and place

the wires inside of seven Toobs. Choose the size that fits the base of the alligator clips. Three inches of wire will protrude from the bottom of each Toob.

11 Poke one wire into the center of each flower on the head. Use a nail to start the holes if necessary.

12 Curl each wired Toob around your finger.

13 Place seven 18-gauge wires into the smallest Toobs. Curl the wired Toobs around your finger. Poke each wire randomly into the head.

14 Punch two suns out of black cardstock, trim in half to form eyelashes, and glue onto face, as shown.

15 Apply two green Biggies sticker leaves over the eyes.

16 Apply one Biggies flower sticker over the lips.

17 Apply one Biggies flower sticker for each ear.

18 Apply the remaining Biggies flowers around the base as if to make a collar.

RESOURCE GUIDE

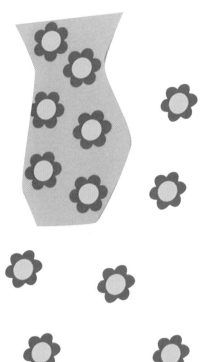

Artistic Wire
752 Larch Avenue
Elmhurst, IL 60126
www.artisticwire.com
Wire

Anna Griffin, Inc.
733 Lambert Drive
Atlanta, GA 30324
www.annagriffin.com
Decorative paper

B & B Etching Products, Inc.
18700 N. 107th Avenue, Suite 13
Sun City, AZ 85373
etchall etching creme

The Beadery
105 Canonchet Road
Hope Valley, RI 02832
www.thebeadery.com
Beads

The Board Dudes, Inc.
2801 Dow Avenue
Tustin, CA 92780
www.boarddudes.com
Bulletin board

Canson, Inc.
21 Industrial Drive
South Haley, MA 01075
www.canson-us.com.
Photo mounting corners

Crafter's Workshop
116 S. Central Avenue
Elmsford, NY 10523
www.thecraftersworkshop.com
Lettering stencils

DCC
428 S. Zelta
Wichita, KS 67207
(800) 835-3013
Papier-mâché products

DMD Industries, Inc.
2300 S. Old Missouri Road
Springdale, AR 72764
www.dmdind.com
Paper Reflections Cardstock
and Creative Tags

Daler-Rowney
2 Corporate Drive
Cranbury, NJ 08152
www.daler-rowney.com
Canford metallic paper

Darice
13000 Darice Parkway
Strongsville, OH 44149-3800
www.darice.com
Craft eyes and wood products

DecoArt
P.O. Box 386
Stanford, KY 40484
www.decoart.com
Paints and finishes

Dowe Chemical Co.
P.O. Box 68
Chagrin Falls, OH 44022
www.styrofoam-crafts.com
Styrofoam products

Duncan Enterprises
5673 E. Shields Avenue
Fresno, CA 93727
www.duncan-enterprises.com.
Glues

EK Success
125 Entin Road
Clifton, NJ 07014
www.eksuccess.com
Zig Memory Systems, Paperkins,
Tracerkins, and Borderbuddies

Eclectic Products, Inc.
995 S. A Street
Springfield, OR 97477
(541) 746-2271
E-6000 glue

Emagination Crafts, Inc.
463 W. Wrightwood Ave.
Elmhurst, IL 60126
(630) 833-9521
www.emaginationcrafts.com
Craft punches, decorative-edged
scissors, Bravissimo! Papers,
handmade papers, eyelets, and
TWISTart paper yarn

Epson America, Inc.
3840 Kilroy Airport Way
Long Beach, CA 90806
www.epson.com.
Stylus Photo Printer, specialty
photo papers, photo stickers, and
photo transfer sheets

Expo International, Inc.
5631 Braxton Drive
Houston, TX 77036
www.expointl.com
Trimatations trim

Fibre-Craft Materials Corp.
6310 W. Touhy Avenue
Niles, IL 60714
www.fibrecraft.com
Creative Hands Foam Flowers

Fiskars Consumer Products
7811 W. Stewart Avenue
Wausau, WI 54401
www.fiskars.com
Scissors, shape cutters, and
decorative-edge scissors

Forster Inc./Diamond Brands
1800 Cloquet Avenue
Cloquet, MN 55720
www.diamondbrands.com
Wood products

Frances Meyer, Inc.
P.O. Box 3088
Savannah, GA 31402-3088
www.francesmeyer.com.
Decorative papers and stickers

MB Glick Co. Inc.
501 Richardson Drive
Lancaster, PA 17603
www.emmascrafts.com
Papier-mâché products

June Tailor Inc.
P.O. Box 208
Richfield, WI 53076
www.junetailor.com
Inkjet printable fabric sheets

Krylon
101 Prospect Avenue NW
540 Midland Building
Cleveland, OH 44115
www.krylon.com
Fixative

Kunin Felt
380 Lafayette Road
Hampton, NH 03842
www.kuninfelt.com
Kreative Canvas II products

The Lacey Paper Co.
22002 Mission Hills Lane
Katy, TX 77450
www.laceypaper.com
Handmade papers

Lara's Crafts
4220 Clay Avenue
Fort Worth, TX 76117
www.larascrafts.com
Wood shapes

The Leather Factory
3847 E. Loop 820 South
Fort Worth, TX 76119
www.leatherfactory.com.
Leather laces and trims

Lenderink Technologies, Inc.
1271 House Street
Belmont, MI 49306
www.lenderink.com
Paper Wood

Mrs. Grossman's Paper Co.
P.O. Box 4467
Petaluma, CA 94955
www.mrsgrossmans.com
Stickers

NRN Designs
5142 Argosy Avenue
Huntington Beach, CA 92649
www.nrndesigns.com
Decorative papers

Paper by Catherine
11328 S. Post Oak Road, #108
Houston, TX 77035
www.papersbycatherine.com
Decorative papers

Provo Craft
151 E. 3450 N.
Spanish Fork, UT 84660
www.provocraft.com
Glass sun catcher, decorative
papers, and stickers

The Punch Bunch
513 Cherokee Drive
Temple, TX 76504
www.thepunchbunch.com
Swirl punches

Syndicate Sales Inc.
2025 N. Wabash Street
Kokomo, IN 46901
www.syndicatesales.com
Plastifoam

Tapestry In Time
www.tapestryintime.com
Power Punch (punch aid)

ThermOWeb
770 Glenn Avenue
Wheeling, IL 60090
www.thermoweb.com
Keep A Memory, Peel n Stick, and
Sticky Dots double-sided adhesive
sheets

Toner Plastics, Inc.
699 Silver Street
Agawam, MA 01001
www.tonerplastics.com
Trims and cords

Walnut Hollow
1409 State Road 23
Dodgeville, WI 53533
www.walnuthollow.com
Wood furniture and
home products

Xyron Inc.
15820 N. 84th Street
Scottsdale, AZ 85260
www.xyron.com
Adhesives

DISCOVER NEW WAYS TO USE YOUR CRAFTING TOOLS

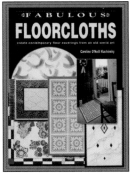

Fabulous Floorcloths

Create Contemporary Floor Coverings from an Old World Art
by Caroline O'Neill Kuchinsky

Contemporary or antique, a floorcloth transforms an ordinary floor into a work of art. The step-by-step instructions guide you through projects easily. Choose designs and color schemes in 14 projects divided into simple to advanced.

Softcover • 8¼x10⅞ • 128 pages
60 color photos • 225 color diagrams
Item# FLODEC • $19.95

Photo Art & Craft

by Carolyn Vosburg Hall

This innovative approach to creative photography and crafting is the ultimate idea book! Filled with foolproof techniques for using tools such as photocopiers and computers, this guide shows you how to turn pictures of your family, friends, pets, landscapes, and special memories into treasured keepsakes and works of art. Includes 50 one-of-a-kind projects, like coasters, blocks, note cards, jewelry, photo grams, a quilt, lampshade, clock, and table.

Softcover • 8¼x10⅞ • 128 pages
250 color photos
Item# PHTC • $21.95

Candle Creations

Ideas for Decoration and Display
by Vivian Peritts

Learn how to quickly and inexpensively change store-bought candles into treasures for your home by using techniques such as adding color, painting, gradation, whipping, softening and twisting. With step-by-step instructions and more than 200 illustrative photographs, you'll be able to recreate the more than 100 beautiful projects with ease.

Softcover • 8¼x10⅞ • 128 pages
200+ color photos
Item# CCIE • $21.95

Shape Your Memories

Creating One-of-a-Kind Scrapbook Pages
by Patti Swoboda

Add new dimension to your scrapbook pages with Patti Swoboda's innovative, new technique! Through step-by-step instructions and photographs, you'll quickly learn how to use common scrapbooking tools and Staedtler's Hot Foil Pen to create shaped pages and page protectors. Features 12 projects and variations, including a bell that can be transformed into a frog, penguin, elephant, monkey, and even a dog! Bonus ideas for using decorative edge scissors are also provided.

Softcover • 8¼x10⅞ • 48 pages
75 color photos & more than 50 full-size patterns
Item# SYM • $10.95

Kids 1st Scrapbooking

by Krause Publications

Share the fun of scrapbooking with kids! Finally, a resource written specifically for children teaches them techniques and page design ideas for scrapbooking. Includes 25 projects with easy-to-follow directions and photos to guide and inspire all ages in the creative process, using techniques such as photo cropping, lettering, rubber stamping, matting, and journaling.

Softcover • 8¼x10⅞ • 48 pages
50 color photos
Item# K1SB • $9.95

Three ways to order

Call 800-258-0929 Offer CRB2

Mail to
  Krause Publications
  Offer CRB2
  P.O. Box 5009
  Iola, WI 54945-5009

Online at www.krausebooks.com

Shipping & Handling: $400 first book, $2.25 each additional. Non-US addresses $20.95 first book, $5.95 each additional.

Sales Tax: CA, IA, IL, NJ, PA, TN, VA WI residents please add appropriate sales tax.